Buddlejas

Royal Horticultural Society Plant Collector Guide

Buddlejas

David D. Stuart

Foreword by Michael A. Dirr

Timber Press

ROYAL HORTICULTURAL SOCIETY

I thank my wife, Ann, for her help, support, patience and proof reading throughout this long project and, of course, I must mention my beloved girls Aimée and Fiona. Thanks also to Dr Gareth Evans for his guidance and support.

Published in association with the Royal Horticultural Society in 2006 by
Timber Press, Inc.
The Haseltine Building
133 S.W. Second Avenue, Suite 450
Portland, Oregon 97204-3527, U.S.A.
www.timberpress.com
For contact information regarding editorial, marketing, sales, and distribution in the
United Kingdom, see www.timberpress.com/uk.

ISBN-13: 978-0-88192-688-0
ISBN-10: 0-88192-688-4

Design by Dick Malt
Printed through Colocraft Ltd., Hong Kong

Library of Congress Cataloging-in-Publication Data
Stuart, David D.
  Buddlejas / David D. Stuart.
    p. cm. – (Royal Horticultural Society plant collector guide)
  Includes bibliographical references and index.
  ISBN-13: 978-0-88192-688-0 (hardcover)
  1. Butterfly bushes. I. Title. II. Series.
  SB413.B86S78 2005
  635.9'3395–dc22
                              2005008020

A catalogue record for this book is also available from the British Library.

Contents

CONTENTS

Foreword

WOW, what a treat to read and admire the photographs in David D. Stuart's classic garden treatise on *Buddleja*. I have always loved the genus and have introduced new cultivars but never fully fathomed the diversity of species until this timely tome. I know David from my travels to English gardens where he always graciously allowed me to study the great national butterfly bush collection at Longstock Park Nursery and gardens. David writes from the perspective of having touched, smelled, and grown the plants. The text is genuine, the observations his, and the resultant whole the most meaningful treatise on the subject. He provides tantalizing tidbits on the naming, history, medicinal uses, and garden worthiness of the species. The cultivar descriptions are the best I have read. This is a book for all gardeners, for *Buddleja* has a place in all gardens. This is the textual and photographic buffet that will fill the souls of all those who love butterfly bushes.

Michael A. Dirr
Professor, University of Georgia

Preface

During the mid-1950s and 1960s my family lived in Aberdeenshire, and as a young boy I was totally ignorant of the existence of the genus *Buddleja*. In 1966 my father's work took the family to Glasgow, where buddlejas grew wild everywhere. I still have a vivid memory of looking through the car window as we drove through the city, in total disbelief at these beautiful flowering shrubs growing from among building rubble, waste ground, and even up high on buildings.

My first-hand experience with the genus came during the early 1970s, when I worked as an apprentice with the City of Glasgow Parks Department in Rosshall Park, a Victorian garden complete with an ornamental lake in the south-west of the city. I arrived in early summer, just in time to see the full glory of the buddlejas. The following spring I was amazed when my journeyman pruned these shrubs down low. I thought that it would kill the poor plants; however, he reassured me that it was for the best. I assisted by removing the debris, muttering under my breath as I spread copious amounts of cow manure. Not long after the poor buddleja massacre, I was amazed at the strength and vigour of growth, the size of the blooms, and their perfume. My journeyman had taught me the importance of correct pruning and feeding to maximize the return from this genus.

My final year as an apprentice was spent at the Glasgow Botanic Garden, where I was introduced to the *Buddlejaceae* and members of the closely related *Loganiaceae*, within which the genus *Buddleja* was once included and which contains *Strychnos nux-vomica*, a very plain glossy-leaved shrub but the first species to make a lasting impression on me. This poisonous plant was in full exposure to the general public, without any warning labels or barriers. One day the assistant curator passed by while I was clearing away some dead leaves. Straight away he informed me about what I was handling, the risks involved, and the symptoms to look for. He then instructed me to wash my hands and all other exposed skin where the leaves might have touched. Later that day, a simple wire screen was erected between the plant and the public and a poison label was put in place. It was after this episode that I took an interest in the medicinal uses of plants; for my Glasgow Parks certificate I wrote my thesis on medicinal plants, of which *Strychnos nux-vomica* took pride of place.

After finishing my apprenticeship in Glasgow I moved to the Royal Botanic Garden, Edinburgh, to study for my diploma in horticulture. Here I encountered many more plants belonging to the *Buddlejaceae* and *Loganiaceae*, both tropical and temperate species. It was not until I was curator at Longstock Park Gardens, Hampshire, that I developed a keen interest in the *Buddleja* species. It all started when a screen of *Rosa* 'Mermaid' started to die off. For many years it had visually sheltered the tennis court and summerhouse from the public visiting the nursery. I needed to replace the screen with something that would be in flower during the tennis season, which usually commenced at the start of Wimbledon in late June. The screen had to be high enough to give a visual barrier, able to cope with the garden's free-draining chalky soils, and drought resistant, as there was no plumbed irrigation. Most importantly, my choice had to be rabbit, hare, and deer proof. From the list of suitable genera, only buddleja fulfilled all the criteria.

The next decision was whether to keep the planting to one sort or to grow a mixture. Thumbing through the *RHS Plant Finder*, I quickly identified several suppliers of buddleja and started buying different species and cultivars. We accumulated more than seventy plants in the first season and planted them out in a large long bed behind the summerhouse. Word got out that we had a bed of buddleja, and it was not long before Peter Short from the National Council for the Conservation of Plants and Gardens (NCCPG) visited the collection. Thanks to his prompting and hard work, the garden became a National Collection Holder for *Buddleja*, and the rest is history.

Prior to collecting all the buddlejas we could get our hands on, I tried to research aspects of the genus. It soon became apparent that there was a huge gap in the reference material on *Buddleja*, with only snippets available in horticultural encyclopaedias, shrub books, and various nursery catalogues. It was when the garden received National Collection status that I really pulled out all the stops to find out more. I visited the libraries of the Royal Botanic Gardens at Kew and Edinburgh, living collections, and herbarium collections. The most useful publication I came across, with descriptions of many buddlejas, was the 1979 monograph *The Loganiaceae of Africa* by A. J. M. Leeuwenberg.

It is my hope that this volume fills that gap for both gardeners and horticulturists alike. In the introduction, I discuss the general characteristics, global distribution, and taxonomic history of the genus. In chapter 1, I provide detailed descriptions of *Buddleja* species; I also discuss plants often mistaken for *Buddleja*. I describe more than 150 *Buddleja* hybrids and cultivars currently available through the trade in chapter 2. In the chapter on care and cultivation, I discuss soil characteristics and amendments helpful in growing healthy plants; proper feeding, pruning, and watering regimes; methods of winter protection; and various pests and diseases as well as organic and biological means for controlling these problems. In chapter 4, I describe techniques for propagating buddlejas from seed and cuttings, various propagation systems, issues of water quality, and micropropagation for both the horticultural industry and home gardener. The text closes with descriptions of butterflies, moths, and other animals that commonly visit buddleja bushes in both the United Kingdom and the United States. Two appendices list public gardens and nurseries with fine *Buddleja* collections and sources for purchasing the plants.

Introduction

The genus *Buddleja* was named in honour of the Reverend Adam Buddle for his outstanding work in taxonomy. Buddle was born in 1665 in Deeping St. James, Lincolnshire, and educated at St. Catharine's Hall, Cambridge University, where he took a degree of bachelor of arts in 1681 and a master of arts in 1685. Buddle collected a vast number of specimens of the British flora, and he amassed thirty-six volumes of herbarium specimen books during the late seventeenth and early eighteenth centuries. Buddle was friendly with John Ray, the author of *A Catalogue of English Plants* (1670). The botanists in Buddle's day used the second edition of John Ray's *Hortus Siccus* (1696) as the standard reference on British flora and as the basis of their taxonomy.

It was through his friendship with Ray that Buddle started on his quest for native mosses and plant species. Volumes 14–36 of his herbarium folios contain his favourite group, the mosses. The specimens are very well laid out, and Buddle provided copious field notes. In 1708 Buddle wrote and compiled an entirely new and complete reference work, *English Flora*, some three years after the death of John Ray. His work showed his high level of accuracy, diligence, and knowledge, and it is a great pity that his flora was never published. Nevertheless, his impressive work with the lower order of plants earned him recognition as an outstanding botanist. Later in Buddle's life, he sent his collection of grasses and mosses to Petiver, Bobart, and Doody (thought to be the best botanist in England at that time), and they were transferred to Tournefort in Paris. Bobart wrote a letter of thanks, dated 4 April 1707, which was inserted between the pages:

> Sir, I am now to be thankful to God and my friends that I have not only seen, but had the perusal of as I think the best collection of its kind in the world, and is as instructive as admirable: if the intellectual is the

best part of mankind certainly whosoever contributes to that is most amiable and performs the greatest part of humanity. I return your Book of Mosses with as many thanks as there [are] leaves among the said Mosses; to which I have sometimes added a plant and sometimes a note, which I offer to your maturer judgment, to be ejected at pleasure; if anything of my endeavours proves pertinent, I have my aim. You will, Sir, easily find my imperfections and defects by this enclosed long Bill [a list of desiderata which accompanies the letter] any of which if to be spared, would prove very acceptable to my small collection, and heartily give thanks that you have been pleased to open our eyes that we may the better discover the wealth of our own country, I being now sensible that we have passed over diverse without sense of distinction. I hope you will safely receive your Book sent by Mrs Bartlet to the Swan at Holborn Bridge carriage paid; and if your candour will prompt you to excuse the Libertie taken by this enclosed note, you will add obligations to, Sir, your most obliged servant, J. Bobart.

Adam Buddle died on 15 April 1715 at the age of fifty. His final resting place is in the graveyard of St. Andrew's Church, Holborn. In his will and testament he left his herbarium collection to Sir Hans Sloane. The work is recognized as Britain's first "national herbarium."

Michael Maunder in *The Plantsman* (1987) states it was Dr. William Houston who first used the name *Buddleja* for some specimens he collected in the West Indies. These species were then seen by Linnaeus, who gave them the name *Buddleja americana*.

This classification of the family *Buddlejaceae* is based on R. K. Brummitt (1992) and D. J. Mabberley (1997). In addition to *Buddleja*, the *Buddlejaceae* includes seven other genera, mostly occurring in warm and tropical climates: *Androya* (one species, Madagascar); *Emorya* (one species, Texas and Mexico); *Gomphostigma* (two species, South Africa); *Nuxia* (fifteen species, southern Arabia and tropical Africa); *Peltanthera* (one species, tropical America); *Polypremum* (one species, warm regions in America); and *Sanango* (one species, Ecuador).

The genus *Buddleja* comprises around a hundred species. A large proportion of species are native to the Americas, from Utah and California to the southern end of South America in Chile and Argentina. Other centres of diversity can be found in Africa (from Arabia to the Cape of Good Hope and over the sea to Madagascar) and Asia (from Nepal through India and

China to Japan). There are no indigenous buddlejas in Australia, regions of the former Soviet Union, or Europe. Four *Buddleja* species have especially wide distributions: *Buddleja americana, Buddleja salvifolia, Buddleja asiatica*, and *Buddleja crispa*. *Buddleja americana* is found in Central America down into the north-western regions of South America. The African species *B. salvifolia* is native from Angola and Kenya in the north down through the eastern countries to Cape Town in South Africa. *Buddleja asiatica* grows naturally throughout eastern India and east into northern and southern China. The final species is one of my favourites, *B. crispa*, which is distributed from Afghanistan east to Kansu Province in China. Many species are very localized and often found in one valley or on one mountainside, such as *Buddleja utahensis*, which grows only in the Washington region of south-western Utah.

Most members of the genus *Buddleja* are fast-growing deciduous and evergreen erect shrubs or small trees. Although there are some herbaceous perennials, in this book I am concerned only with the woody species, some of which can grow up to 30 m (100 ft). Leaves are simple, opposite, or rarely alternate (*Buddleja alternifolia*). In most species stipules form a line joining the leaf bases, although in some species these are absent or reduced. The calyx is four lobed; the corolla is radially symmetric and four lobed, with four stamens. The ovary is superior; the fruit is usually a dry capsule, rarely a berry. New World species tend to be dioecious, whereas Old World species, on the whole, are monoecious.

The majority of *Buddleja* species grow at medium to high elevations and most of the hardy ones are capable of surviving great fluctuations of temperatures and weather conditions, including drought. One such adaptation of hardy species is the hair on the leaves (as well as on the stems and shoots of some). These hairs help to catch moisture from the plentiful supply of mist in their high-elevation habitats, supplementing their water supply. The hairs also reflect sunlight, greatly reducing water loss due to transpiration through their leaves during hot dry sunny days. The root-hardy species, such as *B. crispa*, die off with the mildest of frosts and grow back from the roots.

From an ecological point of view, members of the genus *Buddleja* are colonizers and are well suited to being opportunists. In the wild they do not like direct competition from other trees and shrubs and often grow in forest clearings; at forest edges; and along river, stream, or burn banks on poor, thinly soiled rocky terrain. One of the most successful species adapted to this pioneering way of life is *Buddleja davidii*, whose seeds are tiny, almost the size of ground black pepper, and easily carried in the wind. Once airborne the seeds can be carried great distances in thermals, often being deposited in the most unusual places. In urban settings, *B. davidii* can be found growing in rough poor stony sites such as railway embankments, kerb edges on roadways, demolition sites, and on crumbling masonry. We get glimpses of them peeping up from piles of rubble or clinging to the most precarious, precipitous chimneybreasts, cracked mortar, and gutters. Buddlejas thrive under these seemingly hostile conditions.

From my perspective in the United Kingdom I do not feel that *Buddleja* plants are a threat to the environment; they tend to be short lived in the exposed poor sites which they colonize and they seldom become established in large numbers. However, the states of Oregon and Washington have declared *Buddleja davidii* as a noxious weed and have banned the planting of it in gardens. This law was enacted to protect the environment against this aggressive alien plant. Many more states and countries are showing signs of following their stand against this species. Where germination conditions are good, competition between plants is vigorous and dominant plants shade out the early pioneers such as buddlejas. At the University of Arkansas, Professor Jon Lindstrom is working on *Buddleja* hybrids that are sterile. He is using genetic engineering techniques to produce plants with dwarfed or nonfunctioning reproductive organs or that produce heavier seeds, which are not carried by the wind. For example, one of his crosses involves *B. davidii* and *B. indica*, the end result being a plant with the flowers of *B. davidii* and the heavier seeds of *B. indica*. Through this work, Lindstrom hopes to slow the unwanted spread of the genus into the wild.

Buddleja species and cultivars have become closely linked with butterflies through their popular common name of butterfly bush. In truth many different types of wildlife are attracted to the flowers' sweet nectar. Most people know about day-visiting butterflies, but only a few know about the other nectar-drinking visitors. For instance, during long hot summers, the Longstock collection is regularly visited by the hummingbird hawk-moth (*Macroglossum stellatarum*), which flies in much the same manner as a hummingbird, hovering as it extends its long proboscis to drink up the energy-giving nectar. Hummingbirds (in North America), moths, and other insects can also be drawn into the garden by these beautiful flowering plants.

Chapter 1
Species

Buddleja acuminata

The name comes from the Latin *acumen*, meaning pointed, referring to the pointed tip of the leaf. This species is native to Madagascar and Zaire, where it grows at forest edges and clearings in forests. *Buddleja acuminata* is often found growing at elevations of 500–800 m (1600–2600 ft), where it grows into a large shrub or small tree, often reaching 3 m (9.5 ft) in the wild. The bark is mostly rusty brown when dry. Leaves are opposite and vary greatly in shape; however, they are mainly spear shaped with petioles 0.7–2.0 cm (0.25–0.75 in) long. The flowers are white with erect lobes, small (2 cm, 0.75 in) in diameter, and arranged in short panicles. The flowers are followed by bluish black berries. The seeds are pale brown. This species is not common in general cultivation. USDA zones 5–7

Buddleja agathosma

The species name comes from the old Greek *agathos*, meaning pleasant, and *osma*, smell, referring to the pleasant smell of the flowers. There is a lot of debate among taxonomists regarding this species, and some suggest it should be classified under *Buddleja crispa*. *Buddleja agathosma* is distributed throughout Yunnan Province, China, where it grows at forest edges and woodland clearings. The plant grows into a large shrub or small tree of open habit, often reaching 3.5–5.0 m (11–16 ft), depending on conditions. The leaves have a wavy edge and are large, opposite, variable, and covered in dense silver-grey hairs on both surfaces and stems. The petioles are winged and up to 30 mm (1.2 in) long. Flowers grow in clusters and are small, ranging in colour from lilac to violet and purple-pink, sometimes with an orange throat. The scented flowers are borne in the leaf axils and are followed by a dry fruit capsule. The plant is not altogether hardy in the United Kingdom and is best grown in a sheltered position or against a south-facing wall. During winter temperatures of –7°C (20°F), it can be killed to the ground. My past experience has shown that it breaks from the root from below ground. I kept a few in large pots to overwinter and for display purposes. *Buddleja agathosma* is reasonably common in cultivation. USDA zones 8–10

Buddleja albiflora

Syn. *Buddleja helmsleyana*

The name comes from the Latin *albico*, meaning white, and *flora*, goddess of flowers. It is native to the mountains of central China in Gansu, Guizhou, Henan, Hunan, Shaanxi, Sichuan, and Yunnan Provinces, where it can be found in open woodlands, forest edges, stream banks, and shrub-clad mountainsides at 500–3000 m (1600–10,000 ft) elevation as a shrub or small tree up to 3 m (10 ft) in height. Its leaves are opposite, narrow lanceolate with a long tapered point, and 10–22 cm (4–9 in) long. Branches are cylindrical or quadrangular in profile, smooth, and hairless. The flowers are sweetly fragrant and are borne on long slender tapering panicles 20–45 cm (8–18 in) long; they are produced from midsummer onwards and followed by capsules with brown spindle-shaped seed. Over the years I have found that the plants in the Longstock collection are contrary to the name—the colour is not white but a very pale lilac with orange centres. *Buddleja albiflora* is not common in cultivation. USDA zones 6–9

Roy Lancaster collected a specimen *Buddleja albiflora* (L 1577) from the Zechawagou Valley, Jiuzhaigou, in north-western Sichuan at an elevation of 2800 m (9200 ft). His notes state that it is common in scrub of *Rhododendron*, *Rosa*, *Clematis*, and *Dipelta*. This shrub will reach 2 m (6.5 ft) and has lilac flowers. It has not yet been introduced to the trade.

Buddleja alternifolia

The name comes from the Latin *alterno*, meaning to do in turns, and *folium*, leaf, referring to the alternate arrangement of the leaves, the only example in the genus. The species was originally described and named by Maximowicz in 1880. It is distributed throughout Tibet and China in Gansu, Hebei, Henan, Mongol, Shaanxi, Yunnan, Sichuan, Shensi, and

Shansi Provinces, where it can be found growing along river banks or dried up streams in thickets up to elevations of 1500–4000 m (5000–13,120 ft).

Buddleja alternifolia is a deciduous, vigorous shrub or small tree up to 2–4 m (6.5–13 ft) high, with an open lax habit with fast-growing branches. When the plant grows against a support, it can reach 6 m (20 ft) high. The pendulous tumbling habit makes it look like a waterfall. It has pale brown bark which does not peel until maturity. The young branches are angled to cylindrical in profile. The leaves alternate around the stem and are 3–10 cm (1–4 in) long and 2–13 mm (0.13–0.5 in) wide, lance shaped at the top and broader wedge shaped at the base; glabrous, dull, dark green above, under surface rough sometimes glabrous. Petioles are up to 2 mm (0.13 in) long. The flowers of *B. alternifolia* are slightly fragrant and are produced in densely crowded clusters about 2.5 cm (1 in) wide, often smothering the stem during late spring to early summer and produced from old wood. The blooms are followed by dry capsules with pale brown seeds.

Always prune this species after flowering. This plant is shown off to its best by growing it up a single or multistem specimen to a height of 1.5–2.0 m (5.0–6.5 ft), letting its natural arching habit form a graceful weeping free-flowering bush. The largest specimen of *B. alternifolia* that I have come across is in a private front garden in the Hampshire village of Broughton; I estimate it is about eighty to one hundred years old and still performing well every season. *Buddleja alternifolia* was introduced into general cultivation in 1915 and given the Royal Horticultural Society's Award of Garden Merit in 1993. This very popular species is common in cultivation, and most good nurseries and garden centres stock it. USDA zone 7–9

Buddleja americana

Some authorities classify the following species as belonging to *Buddleja americana*: *B. callicarpoides Buddleja decurrens*, *B. dentata*, *B. floribunda*, *B. occidentalis*, *B. rufescens*, and *B. verbascifolia*. The name *americana* refers to this species' origin in the Americas. It is distributed throughout central Mexico, south to Bolivia and Peru, and is also found on Jamaica and Cuba. *Buddleja americana* is sometimes found in cloud forests in the highlands of Guatemala to sea level in Belize. Its natural habitat is forest clearings along river banks and streams in tropical and subtropical cloud forests. The plant forms a shrub or small tree with leaves that are narrowly ovate to lanceolate, 9–30 cm (3.5–12 in) long, and 2–8 cm (0.75–3 in) wide, with pale stellate tomentose indumentum. The flowers, which appear during mid to late winter, are white with yellow centres and are sweetly scented.

I looked after this species in the glasshouses at the Royal Botanic Garden, Edinburgh, as part of the temperate and tropical collection. Because *Buddleja americana* requires a uniform winter temperature, to achieve ripe enough wood for flowering, it is best suited to a warm glasshouse or conservatory. Several accounts list this plant as being used medicinally to treat skin infections, skin disorders, bruises, and burns by bathing the area in a solution, paste, or extracts made from the leaves. Internally, *B. americana* is used to relieve stomach-aches, urinary infections, digestive upset, and nasal haemorrhages and as a diuretic and heart moderator; it has analgesic properties and somniferous effect. This is the original fix-it-all medicine, and if I owned a hothouse I would seriously consider producing "Stuart's Elixir." Not common in cultivation. USDA zone 9

Buddleja asiatica

The name *asiatica* refers to the plant's origins in Asia; the name was given by Loureiro, who described the species in 1790. *Buddleja asiatica* is distributed from Bangladesh east through Asia into Indonesia; it can be found in India, Bangladesh, Nepal, China, Burma, Thailand, Laos, Cambodia, Vietnam, Malaysia, New Guinea, the Philippines, Hong Kong, and Taiwan. It grows in open woodlands and near coastal regions at elevations from sea level to 2800 m (9200 ft), often found as an understorey shrub or small tree growing up to 7 m (23 ft) in the wild. The young branches are cylindrical with white, grey, or tawny hairs, and the leaves are opposite, up to 30 cm (12 in) long, narrowly lanceolate to ovoid, and densely felted with hairs. Petioles are up to 15 mm (0.6 in) long. The flowers are borne in late winter to early spring on terminal and occasionally axillary shoots in long slender spikes. The blooms are white, pale violet, or greenish and are sweetly scented. After flowering, capsules with pale brown seed are persistent throughout the summer. In the region of origin, the leaves are used as a potent fish poison, and there is reference to its medicinal properties and use in the perfumery industries. *Buddleja asiatica* was introduced into cultivation in 1874 and 1902 and introduced by E. H. Wilson in 1905; it was given a Royal Horticultural Society Award of Garden Merit in 1993. This species is available commercially. USDA zones 9–10

Buddleja auriculata

The name of this species comes from the Latin *auriculata*, meaning ear shaped, referring to the auricles, which join each pair of opposite leaves; with age the auricles wither away. The plant was named and described by Bentham in 1836. *Buddleja auriculata* is widespread throughout South Africa, Zimbabwe, and Mozambique, where it is commonly known as weeping sage, eared buddleja, and treursalie. It is found in rocky ravines on mountain slopes or at the margins of high-elevation evergreen forests. The plant forms a shrub or small tree to 3–4 m (10–13 ft) high, with the lax branches at times almost arching to the ground. The young branches are light brown, rough, and stringy. The leaves are ovate to lanceolate, 3–12 cm (1.2–4.8 in) long and 1–5 cm (0.5–2.0 in) wide, with a tapered point. The colour is glossy medium to dark green above, with whitish grey hairs underneath. The midrib and lateral veins are depressed above and prominent below. Two auricles clasp the main stem. The petioles are hairy and 3–10 cm (1.2–4.0 in) long. The flowers are small, inconspicuous, and vary in colour from cream to flesh, salmon, orange-yellow, and lavender-lilac; they are borne on current year's growth during late autumn to early winter. The stipules are large, leaflike, and conspicuous. Their scent is reminiscent of honey. The flowers are followed by a dry creamy brown capsule which splits into two to four compartments during early summer to early autumn.

The best time to prune *Buddleja auriculata* is during early spring or after it has finished flowering, which will encourage strong vigorous growth. For the best show of these scented flowers, feed them at the same time with a high-potash fertilizer, which will help the plant during the summer to develop flower buds. Use organic mulch around the base such as wood chips, bark, or coconut shells. At Longstock we have grown this species outdoors against a south-facing wall for five years. In my opinion, the flowers are disappointing on showiness; however, they excel in the scent department, filling the air with perfume when most other scented plants either have not started or just finished. During severe winters *B. auriculata* becomes root hardy, vigorously growing away again in the spring. The plant can be given frost protection by mounding up with coarse wood chips, and it will withstand temperatures of 5–38°C (40–100°F). This species is available commercially. USDA zones 9–10

Buddleja australis

The name comes from the Latin *australis*, meaning southern, that is, coming from the Southern Hemisphere. This species was named and described by Vellozo in 1825. In the wild *Buddleja australis* has a wide distribution from southern Brazil to Bolivia, Paraguay, and Argentina; it is also naturalized in Australia, St. Helena, and Réunion. In its natural habitat, the plant grows as an erect shrub or small tree (3.5 m, 11.6 ft) at forest edges and gallery forests growing at elevations of 2000 m (6500 ft). The branches are winged and square in profile; the large opposite serrate leaves are dark green above, grey tomentose beneath, and the venation is conspicuous. When its petioles are present they are broadly winged, connate, and up to 15 mm (0.6 in). The orange or yellow flowers are produced during mid to late autumn in terminal long compact clusters measuring 30 × 2 cm (12 × 0.75 in).

Buddleja australis was collected in 1813 by W. J. Burchell and introduced into cultivation around 1822, when the Royal Botanic Garden, Edinburgh, received seed from a Russian source. At Longstock I grew this species as a specimen plant in a 25-L (15-in) pot in our hardy ornamental nursery shrub compost mix and brought it in for the coldest part of the year, late autumn to midspring. During the summer we placed it in full sun, where it built up flower buds for the autumn. Any pruning should be done after flowering. It should be considered as a specimen best suited to larger frost-free conservatories for its scented, long-lasting flowers. *Buddleja australis* is not common in cultivation. USDA zone 10

Buddleja axillaris

The species name comes from the Latin *axillaris*, meaning standing in the leaf axils. It was described and named by H. B. Willd in 1827. *Buddleja axillaris* comes from southern Africa, Tanzania, the Comoro Islands, and Madagascar, where it can be found growing in forests, often in mountains up to 300–1400 m (1000–4600 ft). It grows as a shrub or small tree up to a height of 3 m (10 ft). The leaves are opposite, and the petioles, if present, are winged and up to 2 cm (0.75 in) long. The scented flowers are white with erect lobes. *Buddleja axillaris* is one of the exceptions to the rule, as black berries are produced as opposed to the usual dry seed capsules. This species is not in common cultivation and is not listed in the *RHS Plant Finder*. USDA zone 10

Buddleja bhutanica

The name refers to the species origin in Bhutan. This species was named and described by Yamazaki. It can be found in central Asia in Bhutan and Lobeysa, where it grows into a shrub 1.5–2.0 m (5.0–6.5 ft) high in brush-scrub on mountains at elevations up to 1700 m (5500 ft). The branches are cylindrical in profile, and the leaves are opposite and perfoliate, meaning that the leaves are clasping or encircling the main stem, an unusual feature of this species. Flowers are white, exceptionally sweetly scented, and produced in terminal panicles followed by a dry persistent brown capsule. *Buddleja bhutanica* is not reliably hardy, but it is suitable for a cool glasshouse or conservatory. Not common in cultivation. USDA zone 9

A specimen of *Buddleja bhutanica* (L 1934) was collected by Roy Lancaster in May 1991 in Bhutan, near Wangdi Phadrong at Mendong, at 1500 m (5000 ft) elevation. His notes show that it is a common shrub growing up to 2 m (6.5 ft) on dry slopes. This form has not yet been introduced to the trade.

Buddleja brachystachya

This species' name is derived from the Greek *brachys*, meaning short, and *stachus*, spear. The plant was named and described by Diels in 1912. This plant is a small shrub growing to a height of 1 m (3.3 ft) in mountains along dry river banks at elevations of 1000–2700 m (3300–8890 ft) in Yunnan Province. Leaf shape and size vary from 1–3.5 cm (0.4–1.5 in) long by 0.5–1.7 cm (0.2–0.75 in) wide, and leaves are covered with grey hairs. The lavender flowers are borne during early spring to early summer in cymes of six to twelve flowers. Not common in cultivation. USDA zone 10

Buddleja brasiliensis

The name comes from the botanical Latin *brasiliensis*, native to Brazil. In the wild the plant makes a large shrub or small tree to 3 m (10 ft). The leaves are oblong to lanceolate and up to 20 cm (8 in) long, with a white hairy under surface. The yellowish orange to reddish orange blooms are borne in many-flowered leafy racemes. *Buddleja brasiliensis* is usually grown under glass in the United Kingdom. In the northern countries of South America, an extract from this plant is used for healing wounds, reducing bruising, and swellings; in Brazil it is used in native medicine as an expectorant. USDA zones 9–11

Buddleja candida

The name comes from the Latin word *candida*, meaning white and shining. *Buddleja candida* was named and described by Dunn and Bull in 1920. It has a wide distribution throughout north-eastern India, southern Sichuan, and south-eastern Xizang and Yunnan, where it can be found at forest edges and alongside streams, ditches, and other water sources growing as a shrub. The young branches are finely hairy. The silvery buff leaves are opposite, 7–18 cm (2.75–7.25 in) long by 1.7–5 cm (0.75–2 in) wide; upper surface becoming glabrous with age and under surface remaining densely woolly. Petioles are 1.5 cm (0.6 in) long and covered in velvety soft hairs. The violet flowers are borne in late summer to early winter in dense drooping terminal panicles up to 20 cm (8 in) long. They are followed by dry brown persistent capsules. To get the best from *B. candida*, prune in spring directly after flowering. Although this species was introduced into cultivation in 1928, it is not common. USDA zones 9–10

Buddleja caryopteridifolia

The name comes from the Greek *karnoni*, meaning a nut, *pteron*, a wing, and the Latin folium, leaf, in reference to the leaf looking like that of a *Caryopteris*. Its distribution is through Yunnan Province and western China. *Buddleja caryopteridifolia* is a deciduous shrub found in rocky ravines on mountain slopes or at the margins of high-elevation forests, where it forms a shrub up to 2 m (6.5 ft) high. Its leaves are opposite ovate to oblong, with large irregularly toothed margins. The lavender flowers are in narrow panicles up to 7.5 cm (3 in) long, produced during early summer. This species flowers on the previous season's wood, so the best results are achieved by light pruning to shape; if the plant becomes messy, however, it can be pruned hard after it has flowered.

W. W. Smith named it in 1916. This species was collected by George Forrest in Yunnan in 1913. Some of his seed collection of 1921–1923 were grown at the Royal Botanic Gardens, Edinburgh, and at Highdown, Sir Fredrick Stern's garden. In these early years a huge argument raged among the aficionados. H. F. Comber suggested that the Highdown plants should be classified as *Buddleja truncatifolia* var. *glandulifera*, while A. D. Cotton suggested they were *Buddleja sterniana*. To confuse matters further, J. Keenan of the Royal Botanic Garden, Edinburgh, placed all the collected plants under various forms of *Buddleja crispa*. The plants in the collection looked nothing like *B. crispa*, and they were more petite than *B. sterniana*. So, until proved otherwise, I will hold out with the name *B. caryopteridifolia* for this plant. Not common in cultivation. USDA zones 8–9

Buddleja colvilei

This species was named by Hooker and Thomson in honour of Sir James Colvile, F.R.S. Its natural distribution is throughout southern Xizan and Yunnan Provinces, Bhutan, India, Nepal, and Sikkim. *Buddleja colvilei* grows on mountains up to elevations of 3660 m (12,000 ft) in the Himalayas, particularly in Sikkim, where it grows as a shrub or small tree in open forests and thickets. In the wild, *B. colvilei* can attain 12 m (40 ft). The leaves are 8–25 cm (3–10 in) long, oval, lance shaped, and tapered at both ends, with shallow teeth on the edges. At first downy above and felted beneath, leaves become dark green and almost glabrous with maturity. During early summer, this species produces flowers on the current season's growth in terminal open pendulous panicles. These are the largest individual flowers of all the hardy buddlejas grown in open cultivation. The crimson or rose-coloured bell-shaped flowers have a white throat, with the four lobes rounded and recurved.

I have had little luck getting *Buddleja colvilei* started and established outside—every fourth or fifth year it is killed by the frosts. If you can get it past this stage, however, the plant is hardy, as I have seen several magnificent mature specimens which have become frost hardy through time. Thus, it is well worth the effort and persistence to establish one. This species is best grown on a free-draining soil with the added protection of a warm wall, and should be protected from winter winds. Pruning is not done annually, owing to the frost cutting this plant down; once established, however, it is best to prune to shape and to restrain after flowering. I agree whole-heartedly with Sir J. Hooker, who once said of the plant "The handsomest of all the Himalayan shrubs." This is another species that I must add to my top ten buddlejas. The plant was introduced into cultivation 1849 and is available at some good nurseries. USDA zones 8–9

In May 1991 a specimen of *Buddleja colvilei* (L 1938) was collected by Roy Lancaster in a forest clearing on a mountain pass at 3300 m (1100 ft) on Phephe La in central Bhutan. There were no flowers present but ample seed from the previous year. In the wild, Lancaster recorded it as a large shrub up to 4 m (13 ft) high. This form has not yet been introduced to the trade.

Buddleja cordata

This name comes from the Greek *cordate*, meaning heart shaped. *Buddleja cordata* is native to Mexico and is found at forest edges and along watercourses in mountains at elevations of 1500–3000 m (5000–10,000 ft). It is a large deciduous shrub to small tree growing to 12 m (40 ft) in cultivation and up to 20 m (65 ft) in the wild. The main stem is furrowed and brownish or blackish. The leaves are opposite and equally paired. The scented flowers are white, creamy, or yellow with a flush of orange at the throat, produced in terminal panicles. They are followed by a dry persistent capsule. Extracts from the foliage, stems, and bark are used in Mexico for treating rheumatism and disorders of the uterus as well as a diuretic. *Buddleja cordata* is not common in cultivation, but there is a very handsome specimen growing in the centenary border in the Sir Harold Hillier Gardens and Arboretum in Hampshire, United Kingdom. USDA zone 8

Buddleja coriacea

This name is from the Latin *corium*, meaning hide, skin, leather, or strap in reference to the texture of the leaves. The species was named and described by Remy in 1847. *Buddleja coriacea* has a wide distribution in Bolivia from La Paz to the shores of Lake Titacaca. It grows at elevations up to 4400 m (14500 ft) in clearings and open areas among scrub, along stream banks, and at edges of woodland. In the wild it is a medium or large sprawling shrub reaching 2–4 m (6.5–13 ft) in height. The small leaves are opposite, thick, and leathery, and the under surface is covered in thick cinnamon brown to fawn-coloured felted hairs. The upper surface is dark green covered in the same coloured hairs, becoming glossy with age. The young shoots and stems are also covered with hairs, which turn a coppery fawn with age and persist for a long time. The scented flowers are borne in terminal clusters and are a rich butter gold to orange-yellow changing to orange-red with age. In Britain this is a shyly flowering species, and it is only during exceptional years that it performs. The foliage is very handsome and when grown well it makes a very attractive foliage plant. Although not totally winter hardy, *B. coriacea* can be kept going through the winter by placing it in a shade or net house or an unheated glasshouse. The most important thing here is to avoid the plant becoming waterlogged and the roots becoming frozen. Not common in cultivation. USDA zone 9

Buddleja crispa

This name is from the Latin *crispus*, meaning curled, wrinkled, in reference to the curled leaf margins. This species was named and described by Bentham in 1835. *Buddleja crispa* is widespread from Afghanistan in the west through Pakistan, India, and Nepal and east to Sichuan, Gansu, Xizang, and Yunnan Provinces in China. This species grows on dry river bottoms and slopes with boulders, on exposed cliffs, and in thickets at elevations of 1400–4300 m (4500–14,100 ft). The plant is a deciduous shrub of spreading bushy habit growing to a height of 5 m (16 ft). The mature growth has cinnamon brown rough and peeling bark; young shoots, leaves, and stems are covered in a thick greyish white hairs, which fade with age to an overall grey colour. The slightly scented lilac flowers appear in early summer and persist to the first frosts. The flowers are produced in terminal panicles measuring 7.5 cm (3 in) long by 5 cm (2 in) wide on the current year's wood. The blooms are followed with dry brown capsules that persist well into autumn.

In 1950 W. J. Bean mentioned that "seed from Dr Aitchison . . . proved perfectly frost hardy for over 30 years." I have found *Buddleja crispa* to be root hardy during the worst winters, shooting away again in mid to late spring—so refrain from digging it up too soon if it looks poorly after the winter. This species responds well to being planted against a warm south-facing wall in a free-draining soil. Whenever this plant was displayed during the flowering period in the summer months, the display always met with the same response from visitors: "What is that beautiful silver and pink plant?!" I usually set it against something which contrasts well with the foliage, such as *Cotinus coggygria* 'Royal Purple' or *Physocarpus opulifolius* 'Diablo'.

Several forms of *Buddleja crispa* are available commercially. Most horticulturists know and grow the low shrubby type; however, in the Royal Botanic Gardens, Kew, next to a gate near the aquatic and grass gardens there is a treelike form which is easily 4.5 m (15 ft) high, with large woolly leaves. I have been assured by Mike Sinnott, the herbaceous and shrub curator, that it is a true form of the species *B. crispa*. He said that in Afghanistan and parts of the Himalayas this species is sometimes treelike in stature and descendants from this arboreal type are still grown in Britain. *Buddleja crispa* was introduced into cultivation in 1850. It is available in some good nurseries. USDA zones 8–9

Buddleja crotonoides

This species' name refers to the leaves, which resemble those of a croton (of the genus *Codiaeum*). It was named and described by A. Grey in 1859. *Buddleja crotonoides* has quite a large distribution from California in the north through the Chiapas highlands of Mexico and the Yucatan countries of Guatemala and Belize south into Honduras, Costa Rica and Nicaragua. In its natural habitat, this species can be found in oak woods and rocky scree, known locally as barrancas, on mountains at elevations of 2000–2500 m (6500–8300 ft), where it grows into a shrub or small tree 2–5 m (6.5–16.5 ft) high. In the wild it is found in association with *Arbutus xalapensis*, *Pinus* species, and *Cratagus pubescens*. The bark is brown and shredding with age, and the young branches are canescent. The notably large leaves measure 4.5–20 cm (1.75–8 in) by 1.8–8 cm (0.75–3 in) and are a main identification factor. The upper and lower surfaces are covered with dense soft hairs, and the petioles are 1.5 cm (0.6 in) long. The inflorescences are 6–18 cm (2.5–7.3 in) long and are in spikes in clusters measuring 0.6–1.2 cm (0.25–0.5 in) in diameter. The greenish white or greenish yellow flowers are borne mainly in winter and spring, and they are followed by dry brown ovoid capsules.

Buddleja crotonoides is another species that needs to be pot grown and brought in for winter protection to maximize its full potential. Once pot grown for three to five years, there might be enough built-in winter protection to plant out in a sheltered spot, provided backup plants are available. Owing to its hardiness rating, this species is not common in cultivation; however, I consider it worth growing as a tender ornamental. USDA zone 9

Buddleja crotonoides subsp. amplexicaulis

The subspecies' name is from the modern Botanical Latin *amplexus*, meaning embrace, encircling, in reference to the base of the leaves. Some taxonomists consider it to be a separate species, *Buddleja amplexicaulis*. *Buddleja crotonoides* subsp. *amplexicaulis* can be found in distinctively different regions from the type species, from Chiapas south to western Guatemala in oak woods and rocky barrancas on mountains at elevations of 2000–2500 m (6500–8200 ft). The plant grows as a shrub or small tree 2–5 m (6.5–16.5 ft) high. The bark is brown, shredding with age, and the young branches are canescent. The leaves are sessile, lanceolate, elliptic or ovate, and 4.5–20 cm (1.75–8 in) long by 1–8 cm (0.5–3.75 in) across. The base of the leaves is amplexicaule, meaning clasping round the stem. The upper surface is stellate-tomentose, sometimes purberulent, and the lower surface has thick floccose tomentum that is 1.5 cm (0.6 in) long. The greenish white or greenish yellow flowers are 6–18 cm (2.5–7.25 in) long, borne in spiked clusters 0.6–1.2 cm (0.25–0.5 in) in diameter. The main flowering period is winter to late spring. Blooms are followed by a dry brown ovoid capsule. The most magnificent specimen of this plant can be found at Greenway Garden in Devon, where it grows in dappled semi-shade on a hillside—the classic buddleja woodland setting. In my experience, *B. crotonoides* subsp. *amplexicaulis* is not winter hardy; I have grown the plant in a large 25-L (15-in) pot, bringing it in for winter protection. Not common in cultivation. USDA zone 9

Buddleja curviflora

This name is from the old Latin *curvi*, meaning curved, and *flora*, flower, in reference to the serpentine form of the flowers spikes. The species was named and described by Hooker and Arnold in 1838. *Buddleja curviflora* is distributed through southern Shikoku, southern Kyushu, and Ryukyu in Japan to Taiwan, where it is found in thickets on stony slopes in lowlands at 100–300 m (330–1000 ft) elevation. It is a deciduous shrub, growing to a height of 1.5–2 m (4–6.5 ft). Its branches are nearly quadrangular and striate, with dense greyish appressed hairs when young becoming brown and hairless with age. The leaves are opposite, widely lanceolate to ovate, 5–15 cm (2–6 in) long by 2–6 cm (0.75–2.25 in) wide. The upper surface is glabrous, and the lower surface almost glaucous. Where a petiole is present, it can reach 5–14 mm (0.25–0.75 in) long. The purple flowers, borne on terminal one-sided spiked panicles measuring 5–15 cm (2–6 in) long, are followed by a small dry brown ellipsoid seed capsule. In China and Japan this plant is used as a fish killer. Although harmless to humans, when a small amount of juice extracted from the leaves is poured into a stream, the surrounding fish die and can be gathered downstream. The Chinese also use it to help treat and clear catarrh. Not common in cultivation. USDA zones 8–9

Buddleja curviflora var. *venenifera* is native to southern Shikoku and southern Kyushu. This variety has a pale brownish hairy under surface to the leaf. Some authorities would rather see this variety classified as *Buddleja japonica*.

Buddleja curviflora f. venenifera

B. Wynn-Jones from Crûg Farm, Gwynedd, Wales, collected a specimen of this plant (B&SWJ 6036) during a visit to the island of Yakushima, Japan. It is similar to the species, but this form has bright purple bowed flowers measuring 10–30 cm (4–12 in) long borne on one-sided terminal panicles. Overall, the plant is a handsome woolly arching plant. It is rare in cultivation. USDA zones 8–9

Buddleja cuspidata

This name comes from the old Latin *cuspid*, meaning narrowing to a sharp point. *Buddleja cuspidata* can only be found in the wild in northern Madagascar, where it grows along river banks and forest edges at elevations of 100–1500 m (330–5000 ft). It grows as a shrub or small tree 3–4 m (10–13 ft) high. The leaves are opposite, ovate or elliptic, and 9–20 cm (3.5–8 in) long by 4–9 cm (1.5–3.5 in) wide. The petioles are usually brown and tomentose, up to 1 cm (0.5 in) long. The yellow flowers are followed by a dry seed capsule. *Buddleja cuspidata* is rare in cultivation. USDA zones 9–10

Buddleja davidii

This species was named in honour of Pére Armand David, a French missionary who made botanical expeditions in China from 1862 to 1873. The species was named and described by Franchet in 1887, and prior to World War II it was known as *B. davidii variabilis*. It is distributed throughout Gansu, Guandong, Guangxi, Guizhou, Hubei, Hunan, Jiangsu, Jiangxi, Shaanxi, Sichuan, Xizang, Yunnan, and Zhejiang Provinces in China, where it can be found among thickets on mountain slopes and on the side of draws in mountains at elevations of 800–3000 m (2600–9850 ft). It has now become naturalized in Japan. This plant is a vigorous deciduous shrub or small tree with an arching habit, growing to 5 m (16 ft) high. The pale brown bark sometimes becomes deeply fissured with age. The branches are quadrangular in profile, and the young shoots are densely covered in felted white hairs which become sparse with age. The leaves are opposite and 7–13 cm (2.75–5 in) long; when young they are sparsely covered with white felt beneath. The scented flowers are lilac purple with orange eyes; they are borne in terminal panicles 9–20 cm (3.5–8 in) long on the current year's growth. The dry brown seed capsules are narrowly oblong and persist to the following year.

Buddleja davidii is one of the hardiest of all the buddlejas, and it withstands severe winters. In addition, it is the plant most associated with butterflies, owing to its ability to freely flower with nectar-rich flowers. It is these characteristics that many plant breeders wish to use when creating new cultivars, and *B. davidii* has provided us with many outstanding garden cultivars. The major down side of the species is its ability to colonize inhospitable wasteland sites; the tiny winged seeds, blown far and wide, are capable of germinating whereverer they settle, be it old tarmac, rubble, or a crevice high on a wall. During World War II it became known as the bombsite plant in Britain, as it was always the first plant to establish itself after an attack. In Oregon *B. davidii* has escaped into the wild and is taking over large portions of the state. Authorities have declared the species and its hybrids noxious weeds, and control measures are in place. *Buddleja davidii* was first recorded at the Royal Botanic Garden, Kew, in 1896, and it was introduced into cultivation in 1890 by E. H. Wilson. The true form of this species is available from a few specialist nurseries. Do be aware, however, that some nurseries will label up any *B. davidii* hybrid that has lost its label just to move it through the gate. USDA zones 5–9

Roy Lancaster collected a specimen of *Buddleja davidii* (L 474) on Mount Omei in western Sichuan in October 1980. He noted that it is a very common species in Sichuan frequenting stony and rocky margins of streams in mountains and stony slopes in scrub. According to Lancaster, the flowers are average in size and colour, nothing special. The plant is growing in the Sir Harold Hillier Gardens and Arboretum in Hampshire, England, and Birr Castle in Northern Ireland. This form has not yet been introduced to the trade.

Buddleja davidii var. alba

The varietal name is from Latin *alba*, meaning white. This plant was named *B. davidii variabilis* var. *alba* by Rehder and Wilson. In this variety all the characteristics of *B. davidii* are present, except that the leaves are narrower and, when young, are more densely white felted above and sparsely so beneath. The leaves are 7–13 cm (2.75–5 in) long, and the flower is white with an orange eye. Although this is a good hardy white variety of *Buddleja*, I prefer *B. fallowiana* var. *alba* because it has stunning grey foliage, a perfect foil for the white flowers. *Buddleja davidii* var. *alba* is available from a few specialist nurseries. USDA zones 6–9

Buddleja davidii var. *magnifica*

Syn. *Buddleja davidii* var. *variabilis, Buddleja variabilis*

The varietal name is from Latin *magnifica*, meaning magnificent. This plant was named and described by Rehder and Wilson in 1909. It has a distribution in the wild similar to that of *Buddleja davidii* and *Buddleja davidii* var. *alba*. The main distinguishing feature of this variety is the overall size of the flower-heads, which are almost twice the length of those of most *B. davidii*. The violet-purple fragrant flowers are borne in terminal panicles 15–30 cm (6–12 in) long.

For sheer volume and show of flowers, this variety should not be overlooked. To me, it has real wow power when grown to its full potential. One of the best specimens of *Buddleja davidii* var. *magnifica* is growing in the Royal Botanic Gardens, Kew. The plant was flowering in its full glory the day I visited, and the blooms were easily 60–75 cm (2.0–2.5 ft) long with some reaching 90 cm (3 ft). I was told this was the result of several factors: early pruning, a warm early spring, a long hot summer, and an autumn feed of potash the previous year, top-dressed with an organic mulch and some fertilizer to boost it in its new growth in the spring. Sadly, this variety is not in common cultivation and it is not listed in the *RHS Plant Finder*. USDA zones 5–9

Buddleja davidii var. *nanhoensis*

The varietal name *nanhoensis* refers to this plant's origin in Nan-Ho Province, China, where it grows in woodland clearings, gullies, and stream edges. It is a small to medium shrub, seldom reaching small tree status. The foliage is very similar to *B. davidii* but the leaf is much narrower and the plant more compact in growth. The flower spikes are showy but smaller than those of *B. davidii*. Over the years, *Buddleja davidii* var. *nanhoensis* has been used to produce new dwarf varieties more suited to the smaller garden. Introduced into cultivation 1914, this variety is available from specialist nurseries. USDA zones 5–9

Buddleja davidii var. *nanhoensis alba*

The varietal name *alba* refers to the white flowers. The distribution and characteristics of this form are identical to *Buddleja davidii* var. *nanhoensis*, and some believe it to be a naturally occurring sport of that variety. This white-flowered form was used in the breeding of the dwarf form *B. davidii* 'White Ball'. It is available at specialist nurseries. USDA zones 5–9

Buddleja davidii var. *superba*

The varietal name is from the Latin *supero*, meaning abundant or to rise above. This variety is native to Yunnan Province in western China. The main difference between this variety and *B. davidii* is the overall size of the blooms. The flower is almost 2.5 times the length of *Buddleja davidii*'s flower, even larger than that of *B. davidii* var. *magnifica*. The violet-purple and fragrant flowers are borne in terminal panicles 20–35 cm (8–14 in) long. *Buddleja davidii* var. *superba* is not listed in the *RHS Plant Finder* and is rare in cultivation. USDA zones 5–9

Buddleja davidii var. *veitchiana*

Rehder named this variety in honour of James Veitch, a British nurseryman and outstanding horticulturist. *Buddleja davidii* var. *veitchiana* has arching branches; the dense flower panicles are a deeper lavender-blue than those of *B. davidii* and have a conspicuous orange eye. This plant was introduced into cultivation by Wilson from his expedition to Hupeh Province in China, and it is noted as being one of the earliest of all the *B. davidii* varieties to bloom. It is not listed in the *RHS Plant Finder* and is rare in cultivation. USDA zones 5–9

Buddleja davidii var. *wilsonii*

This varietal name honours Ernest H. Wilson. This selection has long taper-ing leaves and rosy lilac flowers in lax panicles. The corolla lobes are more or less erect, with crinkled reflexed margins. *Buddleja davidii* var. *wilsonii* is not listed in the *RHS Plant Finder* and is rare in cultivation. USDA zones 5–9

Buddleja delavayi

This species is named in honour of l'Abbé Jean M. Delavay, who collected plants in western China between 1834 and 1895. The plant was named and described by Gagnepain in 1912. Its distribution is restricted to Xizang and Yunnan Provinces, China, where it grows at forest edges, in thickets, and along trails in mountains at elevations of 2000–3000 m (6500–10,000 ft). The plant grows as a shrub or small tree 2–6 m (6.5–20 ft) high and 3 m (10 ft) wide. The young branches and shoots are more or less cylindrical. The leaves are elliptic with wavy margins and/or toothed to entire, opposite, and 4–16 cm (1.5–6.5 in) long; the under surface is densely felted with white hairs. Petioles are usually present and up to 4 mm (0.13 in). The sweetly scented flowers are borne in lax panicles, 4–12 cm (1.5–4.75 in) long, on terminal shoots; they are rose-pink or lavender with an orange eye. The flowers are followed by a dry seed capsule which persists for a long time. Given a sheltered spot, *Buddleja delavayi* will grow well in most sites with free-draining soil and full sun. This species is listed in the *RHS Plant Finder*, although it is not common in cultivation. USDA zones 8–9

Buddleja dysophylla

The name is from the Latin *dyso*, meaning evil or foul smelling, and the Greek *phyll*, leaf. This species is widely distributed from Natal, Transkei, Swaziland, Zaire, and Tanzania to Malawi and Transvaal to the eastern Cape Province. The natural habitat includes forest edges, ravines, or scrub up to 2600 m (8500 ft) elevation, where it is found as a scrambling, straggling, untidy shrub sometimes semi-climbing up to 4 m (13 ft). The bark is pale brown. The young shoots and young branches are quadrangular and covered in a tawny or rusty pubescence, sometimes with thick rusty cream tomentum. The leaves are opposite with petioles up to 30 mm (1.2 in) long. The sweetly scented flowers are white, creamy, greenish, or yellowish, with a maroon throat. They appear from late spring through late summer and are borne in large lax terminal panicles on the current year's wood either in leaf axils or terminally. The flowers are followed by a small seed capsule covered in small brown hairs, which persist through midsummer to midautumn. I did not manage to keep this one alive in the Longstock collection and could not come by a replacement. I expect that care similar to that required by *Buddleja salvifolia* (that is, free-draining soil and frost protection) would be needed, though I feel that it is not as hardy as *B. salvifolia*. *Buddleja dysophylla* is not common in cultivation. USDA zone 9

Buddleja fallowiana

This species was named in honour of George Fallow, a gardener at the Royal Botanic Garden, Edinburgh, from 1890 to 1915 who was killed in Egypt. I. B. Balfour and W. W. Smith named and described the plant in 1917. *Buddleja fallowiana* is common throughout western China, where it can be found in open woodlands, near watercourses, and along forest edges in dappled shade to full sun. This deciduous shrub has an erect compact habit and grows to a height of 1.5–2 m (5–6.5 ft). The young current year's branches are cylindrical in profile; the shoots are densely covered with white hairs. The oblong lanceolate leaves are 10–20 cm (4–8 in) long; mature leaves have felted white hairs beneath and fewer hairs above. The sweetly scented flowers are whitish lavender with an orange throat; they are borne on terminal, erect panicles 20–40 cm (8–16 in) long and appear in midsummer and continue well into the season. The brown dry seed capsule remains on the shoot throughout the winter months.

Normally *Buddleja fallowiana* has a much longer flowering period than *B. davidii*. It is sometimes cut down by hard winter frosts, but this root-hardy plant soon recovers. Gardeners can give extra protection by using a heavy open mulch of coarse wood chips, peat tailings, or bracken around the base. This species is much prized by plant breeders both for its foliage and flowers, and several good hybrids owe their desirable characteristics to this parent. *Buddleja fallowiana* is another on my top ten list. This plant is common in cultivation and is widely available in the trade. USDA zones 8–9

Buddleja fallowiana var. *alba*

This varietal name refers to this plant's white flowers. This plant is very similar to *Buddleja fallowiana*, except for its white flowers, more felted white hairs on the under surface of the leaves, and fewer hairs above on mature leaves. This variety was named by Sabourin in 1929 and was introduced into cultivation in 1925. Like the type species, this variety is sometimes cut down by hard winter frosts but it is root hardy and soon recovers. Gardeners can give extra protection with a heavy mulch of large open wood chips around the base. *Buddleja fallowiana* var. *alba* was given the Royal Horticultural Society's Award of Garden Merit in 1993. It is common in cultivation. USDA zones 7–9

Buddleja farreri

Commonly referred to as Farrer's buddleja, W. W. Smith named this species in honour of Reginald J. Farrer, plant hunter and author. It grows wild in Kansu Province, China. Farrer described its natural habitat by saying, "[it] hugs only the very hottest and driest crevices, cliffs, walls and banks down the most arid and torrid aspects of the Ha Shin Fang." *Buddleja farreri* is a deciduous shrub or small tree growing to a height of 4 m (13 ft). Its branches are covered with soft-felted white hairs, and the leaves are covered with soft-felted white hairs beneath with petioles sometimes winged down the side and up to 5 cm (2 in) long. The rose lilac flowers are borne in panicles produced in clusters up to 20 cm (8 in) long. They appear in midspring on terminal joints on the previous year's growth and are followed by a dry seed capsule.

Buddleja farreri flowers best after a long hot summer, which bears out Farrer's field notes. Because the flowers are carried on side shoots growing from the previous year's wood, this plant should be pruned after flowering in late spring. I have grown this species in a large pot and overwintered it in a heated glasshouse, keeping it on the dry side and only watering when visually under stress. Reginald Farrer introduced the species into cultivation in 1915. It is not commonly available at nurseries and will require some searching. USDA zones 8–10

Buddleja forrestii

This species was named in honour of George Forrest, a plant hunter in China between 1873 and 1932; it was named and described by Diels in 1912. *Buddleja forrestii* has a huge distribution from India through northern Burma, Bhutan, Sichuan, south-eastern Xizang, and south to Yunnan Province in China. It grows in open woodlands, at forest edges, and in stony scrub, chiefly in gullies and along stream or river banks at elevations of

2000–4000 m (6500–13,000 ft). The plant is a deciduous shrub which grows to 1–6 m (3–20 ft) high. The young shoots and branches are quadrangular in cross section, and narrow wings running down the stem are covered in reddish brown hairs which thin with age. The lanceolate leaves are opposite, 5–25 cm (2–10 in) long, and covered in reddish brown hairs only on the under surface, sometimes becoming absent with age. Clear veined ridging appears on the upper surface of the leaf. The flowers are borne on terminal panicles 6–25 (2.3–10 in) by 2–8 cm (0.75–3 in) wide. They are slightly fragrant; range in colour from maroon-orange, mauve, and blue to almost white; and are borne throughout the summer. I personally cannot find a perfume or any kind of smell other than a green plant smell. I have tested several of my friends and they have found a slight scent. The flower is followed by a dry brown seed capsule.

Prune *Buddleja forrestii* in spring. I have grown this species both as root-hardy and pot-grown specimens, and I recommend the latter to be sure of flowering. The specimens grown in open ground always got hit hard by the frost, took most of the summer to make up a sizeable plant, and often never flowered. *Buddleja pterocaulis* is a close relative. This species was introduced into cultivation in 1903, but it is not common in cultivation today. USDA zones 8–9

A specimen of *Buddleja forrestii* (SBEC 173) was collected during the Sino-British Expedition to Cangshan. Roy Lancaster's field notes of May 1981 state, "Large shrub to 4 m [13 ft] high growing on scrubby hillsides in Cangshan of western Yunnan." Roy grew it at his home against a south-facing wall for many years. There is still a specimen growing at the Royal Botanic Garden, Edinburgh. This form has not yet been introduced to the trade.

Buddleja globosa

The species name comes from the Latin *globos*, meaning round, in reference to the globular clusters of flowers. The species was named and described by Hope in 1782. *Buddleja globosa* was the first buddleja in cultivation. Some of the English common names were globose buddlebush and Chilean orange ball tree; today the common name is orange ball tree. It is distributed throughout the Andes in Peru, Chile, and Argentina in forest clearings or forest edges, mainly in mountain regions up to elevations of 2000 m (6500 ft). The plant grows into a large shrub or small tree to 6 m (20 ft). Its leaves are opposite, bullate, and narrowly oblong, 4–24 cm (1.5–9.6 in) long by 1–6 cm (0.5–2.25 in) across, glabrous above, and prominent venation beneath. Petioles are present and are up to 5 cm (2 in) long. The young branches are subquadrangular in cross section. The rich golden yellow, slightly scented flowers are borne on the previous season's growth, in late spring to early summer, in terminal globose inflorescences, followed by a dry capsule with dark brown seed.

Because the plant flowers on the previous season's growth, the best time to prune is directly after flowering. This species is monoecious, with male and female flowers on the same plant. One of the best specimens of *Buddleja globosa* that I have seen was planted on the edge of Harewood Forest, Andover, Hampshire. The woodland planting was facing south-east; it received full morning sun but was shaded from the searing heat of the afternoon. The plant was very healthy, about 3–4 m (10–13 ft) high, with huge leaves and large, rich golden flower-heads. It was obviously very happy in the dappled shade of the woodland edge.

For the last few years the Longstock collection has provided Aston University in Birmingham, England, with *Buddleja globosa* material for their research into chemical compounds from this species. An extract of the plant is giving positive results among sufferers of asthma and other respiratory disorders. In Chile the plant is used as an aid to healing, and in Peru an extract is used to control and eradicate warts. This species was introduced into cultivation by the firm Kennedy and Lee in 1774, and it received the Royal Horticultural Society's Award of Garden Merit in 1993. *Buddleja globosa* is common and is available at any good nursery or garden centre. USDA zones 5–9

A specimen of *Buddleja globosa* (HCM 98017) was recently collected in the wild in Chile. I came across this plant at Pan-Global Plants, a nursery in Gloucestershire. The colour of the flower is a soft cream—different to the usual orange. Overall it grows into a medium-sized shrub and is suitable for a sunny site in any garden soil.

Buddleja glomerata

The species name is from the Latin *glomerata*, meaning collected into rounded heads. It was described and named by H. L. Wendl in 1825. *Buddleja glomerata* is distributed throughout the Cape region of South Africa, where it is found among rocks on hills and mountains in woodland clearings. In the wild it grows to 3.5 m (11 ft), making a small tree or large shrub with a light brown bark covered with a thin layer of bluish scaly hairs. The young shoots, petioles, long midribs, and lateral veins are covered with silvery white, stellate or scaly hairs. The bluish green leaves are oblong to broadly oblong; the upper surface is wrinkled and puckered, with sparse short hairs. The under surface is rusty to silvery white with dense scaly hairs and heavily veined. The petiole measures 0.2–1.3 cm (0.08–0.5 in). The yellowish to bright yellow flowers are borne in terminal spherical heads up to 15 cm (6 in) in diameter from early autumn to early spring. The scent from the flowers is not pleasant and is very similar to that of cockroaches (if you have ever had the misfortune of smelling them). The stipules are large, leaflike, and conspicuous. The fruits are held in a small, creamy brown, hairy, dry capsule, splitting into two to four compartments. *Buddleja glomerata* plants grow well in a well-drained soil and are resistant to drought, heat, and cold. They root easily from cuttings. It is listed by a few nurseries in the *RHS Plant Finder*. USDA zone 8–9

Buddleja heliophila

The species name is from the Greek *helio*, meaning sun, and *philus*, loving. This species was named and described by W. W. Smith in 1913. *Buddleja heliophila* is distributed throughout Yunnan Province in western China and was first collected by George Forrest. As its name suggests this plant loves the sun and grows as a deciduous shrub or small tree to 3.5 m (11.5 ft) in open sunny sites at forest edges and clearings at elevations of up to 3050 m (10,000 ft). The young stems and shoots are cylindrical in cross section and covered in greyish woolly hairs. The leaves are elliptical or lanceolate; the under surface is covered with soft yellowish to greyish felted wool, and the upper surface is almost glabrous. The petioles are up to 5–6 cm (2–2.3 in) long. The rose-lavender flowers are borne on small branched panicles 7–15 cm (2.75–6 in) long; they are produced on the previous season's growth in late spring on short, often leafy shoots. The flowers are quite fragrant and are followed by dry fruit capsules containing pale brown seeds.

Though *Buddleja heliophila* is regarded as root hardy, I found that it often succumbed to our mild winters and would take most of the summer to make up again. Success was only achieved by growing the plant in a large pot and giving it winter protection. Occasionally, if the summer suits, *B. heliophila* will flower for a second flush in the autumn, when terminal panicles are produced on the current season's growth. The taxonomist A. J. M. Leeuwenberg classifies it under *Buddleja delavayi*. In my opinion, however, the plant sourced for the Longstock collection was different from *B. delavayi* and will be classified as *B. heliophila* until further proof is gathered. This species was introduced into cultivation in 1913. This plant is listed in the *RHS Plant Finder* under *B. delavayi*. USDA zone 8

Buddleja indica

Syn. *Nicodemia diversifolia*

The species name is from the Latin word *indicatio*, meaning indication. The plant was named and described by Lamarck in 1798. It is commonly known as the indoor oak and is distributed on Madagascar, Comoro, and the Mascarene Islands. In its natural habitat, *Buddleja indica* grows into a shrub up to 4 m (13 ft) with its shoots climbing or trailing; it ranges from the coast to the mountains at elevations up to 2000 m (6500 ft) in either scrubby bush or open places. The leaves are smooth, dark green, opposite, and are generally evergreen; the shape varies from orbicular (5 × 5 cm, 2 × 2 in) to resembling that of an oak leaf (5 × 14 cm, 2 × 5.5 in) in shape with variable margins. Petioles are sometimes present and range 3–10 mm (0.13–0.33 in) long. The small flowers are greenish yellow, yellow, to white in colour. Seeds are dark brown and produced within a white or yellowish berry rather than a capsule.

I have grown *Buddleja indica* for six years now and, even with winter protection, have never seen it flower. I have concluded that it will only perform in a subtropical or tropical glasshouses of a botanical garden. The plant requires a minimum temperature of 18°C (64°F) with high humidity. I strongly advise winter protection and keeping the soil on the dry side for optimum survival. If the temperature falls below 5°C (41°F) defoliation can be expected, and if it falls slightly below 0°C (32°F) then there is little chance of a recovery. In my opinion this is a great tender foliage plant and well worth having in the collection. In warmer climates this plant is often grown as a decorative foliage plant for use in conservatories and hothouses. It is sometimes sold under the name *Nicodemia diversifolia*. Not common in cultivation. USDA zone 10

Buddleja japonica

The botanical Latin name *japonica* refers to the species' origin in Japan. This species was named and described by Hemsley in 1889. Its distribution is from Honshu to Shikoku in Japan, where it is found growing on sunny, stony slopes at elevations of 600–1600 m (2000–5300 ft). The plant is a sparsely branched deciduous shrub with open habit, growing up to 1 m (3 ft) in cultivation and 1.5 m (5 ft) in the wild. The current year's branches are stiff, quadrangular in cross section, and narrowly winged on the ridges; young growth is densely felted white, becoming brown with age. The leaves are opposite, 6–20 cm (2.5–8 in) long, dark green and glabrous above, at first tawny felted beneath. The purple, pale lilac, and lavender flowers are borne on terminal, one-sided, drooping panicles measuring 6–15 cm (2.5–6 in) long by 2.5–6 cm (1–2.25 in) wide. Blooms are followed by dry egg-shaped fruit capsules.

There is little about this species to win over gardeners, except when a mature plant is covered with masses of berries in autumn. *Buddleja japonica* is relatively short-lived as a garden plant, owing to the abundant seed produced, and a collection should be renewed regularly with young plants. I also recommend deadheading to extend the life of this plant. Altogether, I have had little success in getting it to establish as an open-grown plant and can only manage to keep the stock plants as pot-grown specimens with winter protection. In *Trees and Shrubs Hardy in the British Isles*, W. J. Bean recommended that this species should be grown from seed; however, we have not found any major problems with vegetative propagation. In the *Flora of Japan* Watsuki et al. noted, "The white flowered form has been named *B. albiflora* Akasaawa." *Buddleja japonica* was introduced into cultivation in 1896. It is available in the nursery trade. USDA zones 8–9

Buddleja limitanea

The species name is from the Latin *limitinis*, meaning bounded or enclosed with limits. *Buddleja limitanea* was described and named by W. W. Smith, although Diels placed it under *Buddleja forrestii* as a synonym. Its distribution is in Yunnan Province in China and Burma, where it can be found in open woodlands, on the edge of forests and dense woodlands, and in rough scrub near streams and river banks. *Buddleja limitanea* is usually found high in the mountains at elevations of 2700–3600 m (8800–12,000 ft). Its natural habit is that of a large, vigorous lax shrub or small tree up to 11–16 m (36–52 ft) with a spread of 2–6 m (6.5–20 ft). The flowers are red to dark salmon pink in 6–20 cm (2.5–8 in) long, terminal panicles.

My original stock in the Longstock collection was kindly supplied by the Royal Botanic Garden, Edinburgh, and it took me a long time to track it down. Once the plant took its place in the collection, I managed to bring it to flower and then disaster hit—the plant keeled over and died within a matter of days. I was terribly upset to admit having killed the only *Buddleja limitanea* plant in the United Kingdom outside of Edinburgh. On a visit to Greenway Garden in Devon, prior to it being bequeathed to the National Trust, I spied one lopsided specimen lurking in the background, which, though reluctant, they did sell to me. *Buddleja limitanea* is not common in cultivation. USDA zones 8–9

Buddleja lindleyana

In 1844 Fortune named this species in honour of Dr. John Lindley (1799–1865), professor of botany and secretary of the Royal Horticultural Society. *Buddleja lindleyana* is a native of Sichuan, Hupeh, Kiangsu, Anhwei, Shanghai, Hunan, and Yunnan Provinces in China and has become naturalized in Okinawa-jima, Japan. There have been reports of this species naturalizing in the south-eastern United States as well. George Forrest collected it from a garden on the island of Chusan, and it was introduced into cultivation in 1843 by Robert Fortune. In its natural habitat, this species can grow to a height of 1–3 m (3–10 ft) and grows in rocky scrub beside trails and streams and in forest edges at elevations of 200–2700 m (650–8800 ft). This shrub has slender branches; the young shoots are quadrangular in cross section and narrowly winged on ridges. The opposite dark green leaves are 4–20 cm (1.5–8 in) long, ovate, and tapered towards the apex; they are almost hairless above, with rusty hair beneath. During late spring to midautumn, the deep red or violet-purple flowers are borne in terminal, slender, one-sided spiked panicles measuring 10–30 cm (4–12 in) long. Sadly, the flowers have no scent. Flowers are followed by small dry brown seed capsules.

In China the leaves of *Buddleja lindleyana* are used as a fish intoxicating herb, which aids in harvesting of large quantities of fish. This species is best grown against a warm south-facing wall or sheltered shrubbery. A mature plant of this species is growing at Bath Botanic Garden; it has reached a height of 4 m (13 ft) and has come through numerous winters. One of the best examples is in the Sir Harold Hillier Gardens and Arboretum in a mixed border, giving it added protection from cold winter winds. This plant should be pruned in the spring if required. It is reasonably common in cultivation and available through good specialist nurseries. USDA zone 8

In June 1993 Roy Lancaster collected *Buddleja lindleyana* f. *sinuato-dentata* (L 2024) on the road to Boaxing, western Sichuan, at 900 m (3000 ft) elevation. His notes described it as "a shrub up to 2 m [6.5 ft] in height, leaves have bold teeth along edges, growing in rock crevices in shady gorge." Roy informs me that there is a plant growing with Richard Duke, Ampfield, Romsey, Hampshire. This form has not yet been introduced to the trade.

Buddleja loricata

Syn. *Nuxia corrugata* and *Chilianthus corrugatus*

The name is derived from Latin *lorica*, meaning breastplate, referring to the shape of the leaf. It was named and described by Leeuwenberg in 1975. *Buddleja loricata* is distributed throughout South Africa and Mozambique, where it grows among rocks or in moist sheltered places on slopes of high mountains above 1800 m (6000 ft). The plant grows into a bushy shrub to 4 m (13 ft) and has pale brown peeling bark. The evergreen leaves are opposite, narrowly oblong elliptic, and 1.5–9 cm (0.6–3.5 in) by 0.2–2 cm (0.13–0.75 in) wide. The upper surface is medium to dark green, wrinkled, and puckered; the under surface is covered with dense rusty hairs and heavily veined. The petiole is hairy and up to 1.3 cm (0.5 in) long. The flowers are cream, sometimes with an orange throat, borne in clustered terminal heads from midautumn to early winter. Anthers protrude from the mouth of the flower. The flower is scented; some people think it smells sweet like honey, while others find it to be unpleasant. The small ovoid seed capsule is covered in dense creamy grey hairs; from midwinter to early spring it splits with age into two to four compartments, revealed in dense woolly heads.

Buddleja loricata is one of my favourite buddlejas because it has interest all year round. It is compact and evergreen. The species is very easy to grow in a well-drained soil and is resistant to drought, heat, and cold. In the Longstock collection the plant proved to be hardy and evergreen, with the older leaves persisting into midsummer. Very little pruning is required and is only recommended for shaping if required. *Buddleja loricata* is another one of my top ten favourites. It is reasonably common in cultivation and should be available at specialist nurseries. USDA zones 7–9

Buddleja macrostachya

This species' name is derived from Latin *macro*, meaning large, and *stachya*, spike-shaped, referring to the size and shape of the inflorescence. The species was named and described by Wallich ex Bentham in 1835. *Buddleja macrostachya* has a widespread distribution in India; Bhutan; Bangladesh; Burma; Thailand; Vietnam; Yunnan, Guizhou, and Sichuan Provinces of south-western China; Macao; Hong Kong; and Japan. In China it is locally known as *Da xu zui yu cao*, which translates as "fish intoxicating plant". The plant is a deciduous large shrub or small tree, 1–6 m (3.25–20 ft) tall, with an upright, loose, open, coarse habit. When pruned in the spring, it can grow to 2–3 m (6.5–10 ft) in the season. The leaves are opposite, 25 cm (10 in) long, with narrowly sometimes broadly elliptic margins scalloped or toothed. The under surface is densely felted with white hairs; the upper surface is almost hairless and dark green. Branches are often four-winged and densely felted with white hairs. Flowers appear very late in the season and are only borne during a good hot summer; they are mauve, purple, pinkish, lilac, or occasionally creamy white with an orange to red throat, and held in terminal spikes. The seed is pale brown and winged at both ends.

Buddleja macrostachya is not altogether hardy and is best grown against a wall or brought inside for winter protection. Overall this is a plant more suited for a collection of *Buddleja* or large foliage plants. It is available from specialist nurseries. USDA zones 9–10

Buddleja macrostachya (Heronswood Nursery form) was collected in China by Dan Hinkley of Heronswood Nursery, U.S.A., and is sold through Pan-Global Plants from Gloucestershire in the United Kingdom. It is a large fast-growing shrub suitable for sheltered gardens. The sweetly scented, lavender tinged, creamy white flowers with orange throats are arranged in cylindrical panicles and appear during midsummer.

Roy Lancaster collected a *Buddleja macrostachya* specimen (SBEC 360) on the Sino-British Expedition to Cangshan in 1981. I remember seeing this plant for the first time growing against the south-facing wall of Roy's two-storey house in Chandlers Ford. Until that time I never knew that buddleja could grow to such proportions. It towered above the house and the leaves were massive. To me this was the beanstalk from "Jack and the Beanstalk" of the buddleja world. Roy collected it on the western flank of Changshan, where it grows in forest clearings into a large shrub or small tree of 4–5 m (13–17 ft). Roy noted, "Shoots four-winged, large green leaves, swan neck slender inflorescences with disappointingly small flowers. Resembles a more robust version of *B. forrestii*." I am unsure of any surviving plants from this collection—Roy had to save his house from the giant and a large specimen growing in the Chelsea Physic Garden, in London, had to be destroyed due to its vigour. This form has not yet been introduced to the trade.

Buddleja madagascariensis

Syn. *Nicodemia madagascariensis*

The species name refers to its place of origin, the island of Madagascar. Some authorities place *Buddleja heterophylla* in with this species. *Buddleja madagascariensis* has become naturalized in Fujian, Guangdong, and Guangxi Provinces in China, is in cultivation throughout tropical and sub-tropical Asia, and has become naturalized along the Mediterranean coast of France. This species was named and described by Lamarck in 1792. The plant grows among bush scrub in mountains at elevations of 600–2000 m (2000–6500 ft), where it is a vigorous, loose, lax semi-evergreen to evergreen shrub to 4 m (13 ft). Its leaves are opposite or sometimes subopposite, 4–12 cm (1.5–5.75 in) long, and narrowly ovate. They are dark green above with impressed reticulate venation, densely felted with white or grey hairs; hairs are dry and rust coloured beneath. Petioles are 5–20 cm (2–8 in) long. When young, shoots and branches are covered in white tomentose, ageing to rusty red-brown. The dark yellow, orange, or salmon flowers are produced on terminal panicles up to 25 cm (10 in) long. The flowers are exquisitely fragrant and are followed by a blue, violet, or orange berry with medium brown seed.

Buddleja madagascariensis is a worthy species and would be a good choice to grow in a large conservatory or against the warmest wall in the garden, where the temperature does not drop below 2°C. This species is only hardy if given extra frost protection (such as an extra-thick layer of chunky mulch and fleece or water-pipe lagging foam over the main stem) or brought in for the winter. It is a popular choice among landscape designers in California to hide or cover unsightly objects. Prune it in the spring to shape, if required, or after flowering. *Buddleja madagascariensis* received the Award of Garden Merit from the Royal Horticultural Society in 2002. It is rare in cultivation. USDA zones 9–10

Buddleja marrubiifolia

The name is believed to have its roots in the old Hebrew word *marrubium*, one of the five bitter herbs eaten by Jews at the feast of Passover, and the Latin *folia*, leaf. In North America it is known as the woolly butterfly bush. It is found in the Chihuahuan Desert from Texas to New Mexico and from Chihuahua south to San Luis Potosí, where it grows in limestone canyons, arroyos (narrow gorges), and rocky slopes. This round shrub grows to 1.75 × 1.75 m (5.8 × 5.8 ft) and is covered in white hairs. The scented flowers are orange and arranged in marble-sized terminal and axillary spheres. The plant flowers in the spring and again in the autumn.

The important thing that this plant needs to grow is a very, very free-draining soil, such as the crushed brick mixture described in chapter 3, and full sun. This plant will cope with a huge variation in temperatures and is well adapted to desert conditions, in which temperatures can go from 40°C to −10°C (104 to 14°F) in one day. *Buddleja marrubiifolia* is rare in cultivation. USDA zone 7

Buddleja myriantha

The name is derived from the Greek word *myrios*, meaning myriad, and *anthos*, flower. This species was named and described by Diels in 1912. *Buddleja myriantha* has a wide distribution from northern Burma through south-western China in Gansu, Guangdong, Guizhou, Hunan, Sichuan, Xizang, and Yunnan Provinces and well into Tibet. In the wild plants grow along forest edges, in rocky woodland clearings, in thickets, and along stream banks at elevations of 400–3400 m (1300–12,000 ft). This deciduous shrub reaches a height of 3 m (10 ft). The young shoots and branches are quadrangular, sometimes winged, with sometimes densely felted white hairs. The opposite leaves are narrowly elliptic to lanceolate, 7–14 cm (2.8–5.6 in) long, and densely felted with white hairs beneath. The upper surface is dark green and devoid of hairs. The purple-violet or white flowers are borne in terminal cylindrical inflorescence 6–22 cm (2.5–8.8 in) long during the summer; they are followed by a dry brown capsule.

Buddleja myriantha in the Longstock collection was always grown in a pot and given winter protection to achieve good results with flowering. I have never tried it outside, but I see no reason that it would not survive Britain's winters. It will withstand temperatures down to −12°C (10°F) if planted in a free-draining soil. I found that this species gave off some kind of a dust that made me cough for the best part of half an hour, even with a large drink of water to help clear my throat. The dust also has an effect similar to itching powder. This buddleja is often mistaken for a *Phlomis* due to the similarity of the leaf structure and leaf hairs. It is rare under cultivation. USDA zone 8

Buddleja nappii

This species was named by Lorentz in 1881 in honour of Richard Napp, an important naturalist in the early years of the Argentinean Republic. It is native to the steppes and semi-deserts of Patagonia, southern Mendoza to Rio Negro and Neuquen Province in Argentina, and Chile, where it grows in dry stony sunny clearings near streams. In the wild *Buddleja nappii* is a large shrub or small tree up to 3 m (10 ft). This evergreen has long narrow leaves up to 15 cm (6 in) long and 2.5 cm (1 in) broad, pointed at apex and blunt at the base. The stems have pale brown bark, peeling into strips with age. The orange flowers are borne in terminal inflorescences in three to eight terminal, globose, pedunculate heads 1–2 cm (0.5–0.8 in) in diameter. They are followed by a dry seed capsule, usually with infertile seed. Flowering period is early summer, slightly later than *B. globosa*. Unlike most New World species, plants are monoecious, with male and female flowers on the same plant.

I was unsure about the validity of this species due to what little information is available. At every opportunity, however, I checked stock plants at nurseries and in other collections. All looked like a slender form of *Buddleja globosa*, with the flowers, leaves, seed heads, and overall size being smaller in *B. nappii*. In addition, *B. nappii* has a distinctive, almost shiny, coppery tone on the under surface of the leaves, as opposed to the matted pale grey of *B. globosa*. I now tend to use this characteristic as a way of identification. *Buddleja nappii* is not common in cultivation. USDA zones 7–9

Buddleja nivea

This name is from the Latin word *nivalis*, meaning snowy or snow white, in reference to the white felt covering the shoots, stems, and leaves. This trait is typical of xerophytes (plants which grow in extreme dry-weather conditions), as it helps slow transpiration from the leaf and helps trap moisture from the low mountain-induced clouds. The species was named and described by Duthie in 1905. *Buddleja nivea* is narrowly distributed in the Yangtze River basin in Sichuan, Xizang, and Yunnan Provinces in China. It grows in open woodland, along river and stream banks, at forest edges, and in thickets on mountains at elevations of 700–3600 m (2300–12,000 ft). The plant grows as a shrub 1–3 m (3–10 ft) high. Leaves are lanceolate, 4–15 cm (1.5–5 in) long, hairy above, greyish yellow beneath. Young shoots and stems are densely covered in grey woolly hairs which persist for some time. The purple or violet flowers are small, with erect lobes resembling ears, and are arranged in compound panicles 5–15 cm (2–6 in) long. Some people say it is very slightly scented. I keep hoping that I might get lucky and smell it. Ah well, there is always next year. After flowering the dry seed capsules persist for some time; they look unsightly and are best removed.

In the wild *Buddleja nivea* is an evergreen shrub, but it sometimes is deciduous if grown in the open in Britain. At Longstock we did manage to keep it evergreen by bringing it in for winter protection. This species is not recommended for its flowers, as they are small and insignificant. However, it is the buddleja with the most outstanding foliage—the entire plant is clothed in white felted hair. If pruned throughout the summer to remove the flowers, the white foliage effect is improved for the winter months. Leeuwenberg noted that it is closely allied to *Buddleja candida*. It is in general cultivation and should be available from specialist nurseries. USDA zones 7–8

Roy Lancaster collected a specimen of *Buddleja nivea* (L 815) on steep slopes in scrub on the road between Yaan and Han Yuan at 2400 m (7800 ft) elevation in western Sichuan. In his notes he described it as "a shrub growing to 2.5 m [7 ft] high. A densely grey downy plant with tiny flowers in dense tail like inflorescences." To me this is the best form of *B. nivea* and I am pleased to see it becoming more widely available throughout the nursery trade. Planted in the right place, such as in front of an evergreen or dark background, the white-felted foliage and shoots stand out like a ghostly beacon.

Lancaster collected another specimen of *Buddleja nivea* (L 860) on the road between Luding and Kangding in western Sichuan at 2000 m (6600 ft) elevation. His notes describe it as "a shrub up to 2 m [7 ft] high on rocky slopes in gorges." He questions the identity and offers *Buddleja stenostachya* as the correct name. The original plant is still grown in the Sir Harold Hillier Gardens and Arboretum. This form is not yet available in the trade.

Buddleja nivea pink-flowered

The distribution of this form is relatively unknown; however, I understand that it is from Yunnan Province in China. Its habitat is similar to *Buddleja nivea*: in open woodland, at forest edges, and in thickets on mountains at elevations of 700–3600 m (2300–12,000 ft). It grows as a shrub 1–3 m (3–10 ft) high. Leaves are very similar to *B. nivea*, however the young shoots and stems are not as densely covered in grey woolly hairs. Flowers are numerous and grouped in tight flower panicles 5–30 cm (2–12 in) long; the individual flowers are small and pink-lilac with erect lobes. After flowering the dry seed capsules persist for some time and look unsightly. Although this form produces more flowers than the type species, I would not recommended it for its flowers, as they are small and insignificant. USDA zones 7–8

Buddleja nivea var. *yunnanensis*

This variety is native to Yunnan Province in south-western China. It was named and described by Rehder and Wilson in 1913. *Buddleja nivea* var. *yunnanensis* is a vigorous deciduous shrub to small tree, reaching 4 m (13 ft) in cultivation. Every part of the young shoots are covered with white hairs, although fewer than on *B. nivea*. The leaves are opposite and much larger than the species, 20–50 cm (8–20 in) long, ovate lanceolate, and wedge shaped. The under surface is felted with yellow brownish hairs. The violet-purple flowers are in inflorescences and again are much larger than species. They are followed by a dry seed capsule.

Buddleja nivea var. *yunnanensis* is one of the most vigorous plants in the Longstock collection and produces leaves in excess of 50 cm (20 in). When pruned in the spring to 30 cm (12 in) from the ground, this variety will grow to 3 m (10 ft) plus in a good season. Due to its vigour, I would recommend that it be confined to large gardens, where it can be grown and shown to its best. It is best grown in full sun and in a free-draining soil. This variety is not common in cultivation. USDA zones 7–8

Buddleja officinalis

The species name is from the Latin *officium*, meaning of the service, official duty, or function, referring to the usefulness of the plant as a source of dye, food, medicine, and perfume. First discovered by Dr. Pavel Piasetski, a surgeon in the Russian army, in 1875; this species was named and described by Maximowicz in 1880. *Buddleja officinalis* is distributed over a wide area in Hupeh, Shensi, Anhui, Fujian, Gansu, Guangdong, Guangxi, Guizhou, Henan, Hubei, Hunan, Jiangsu, Shaanxi, Shanxi, Sichuan, Xizang, and Yunnan Provinces in China, Myanmar, and Vietnam. It grows at elevations of 200–2800 m (650–9200 ft) along woodland edges, in clearings, and along river and stream banks. The plant is an evergreen upright shrub, 1.5–2 m (5–6.6 ft); sometimes it becomes deciduous when grown in the open in Britain. The leaves are lanceolate, 4–15 cm (1.6–6 in) long, hairy above, and greyish yellow beneath. Young shoots and stems are densely covered in grey woolly hairs which persist for some time. The flowers are borne in terminal panicles in clusters of three to ten spikes per panicle; they are a soft lilac-mauve with a pink, sometimes an orange, throat, and sweetly scented, almost like hyacinth but stronger. The corolla tube is about four times as long as it is wide. The fruits are dry brown seed capsules which persist well into the next season.

Buddleja officinalis is a winter-flowering species; it usually flowers around Christmas and continues well into midspring. This outstanding species should be seriously considered for growing as a conservatory plant or as a specimen against a warm wall or in a very sheltered spot in the garden. The perfume from this plant will easily outperform the powerful scents of hyacinth and jasmines. I would definitely put this species on my top ten list, and when I have a conservatory I will definitely own one of these beauties. During the summer months the plant can be put outside, bringing it back indoors for the frosty months. I have managed to keep it evergreen by bringing it in for winter protection. Prune *B. officinalis* in the spring after flowering if required. Every three to four years it pays to prune heavily to regenerate the vigour and increase flower production. The merits of *Buddleja officinalis* were first recognized by the Royal Horticultural Society as early as 1911, when a plant was exhibited by the Veitch Nursery. More recently it has received the Royal Horticultural Society's Award of Garden Merit in 2002. This species is reasonably rare in cultivation and needs to be promoted. USDA zones 8–9

Roy Lancaster collected a specimen of *Buddleja officinalis* (L 1830) in a gorge above the Daning River, a tributary of the Yangtze River, west of Yichang in western Hubei. His notes say that it "grows to a height of 2.5 m [8 ft] on sunny dry steep slopes. Flowers during the winter, and has bold panicles of richly fragrant flowers." Material from this specimen is available in the nursery trade and it makes a super plant for the conservatory. Grow it outside in the summer and bring it in for the winter. In sheltered gardens it can be grown against a warm south-facing wall.

Buddleja officinalis f. albiflora

This is a white-flowered form of *Buddleja officinalis*; all traits are the same as the type species but the flowers are white. This form is very rare in cultivation. USDA zones 8–9

Buddleja paniculata

Syn. *Buddleja acutifoila, B. lavandulacea, B. gynandra, B. mairei, B. mairei albiflora*

This species' name comes from Latin word *panicula*, meaning tuft, and it was named and described by Wallich in 1820. *Buddleja paniculata* has a wide distribution from northern India to Bhutan, where it can be found growing at forest edges, in open woodlands, in thickets, and among rocky slopes at elevations of 500–3000 m (1640–9800 ft). The plant grows as a large shrub or small tree to 6 m (20 ft) in height. It is deciduous and has leaves that are opposite and covered in fine grey hairs. The flowers are sweetly scented, pale lilac, and borne in terminal panicles. This species is dioecious, that is, a plant produces either male or female flowers.

At Longstock I used our standard hardy ornamental nursery stock loam-based compost to grow *Buddleja paniculata* with good results. Winter protection in a cool frost-free glasshouse is given to the specimen plants prior to first frosts and the soil is kept on the dry side. I strongly recommend this buddleja for a conservatory as it usually flowers soon after Christmas and continues well into midspring. The flowers easily outperform the powerful perfumes of hyacinths and jasmines. In Yunnan Province, this species is used for soil stabilization as it forms a large fibrous root mat and is quick growing—it is a first-class pioneer plant. *Buddleja paniculata* is not common in cultivation but should be sought. USDA zone 8

Buddleja parviflora

This summer-flowering species is native to Mexico, where it can be found in open scrubland at woodland edges and alongside river and stream beds. Some authorities classify this as *Buddleja microphylla* (HBK). The plant is a shrub or small tree growing to a height of 5 m (16 ft). The leaves are opposite, woolly beneath, and almost hairless above. New shoots are also covered in woolly hairs that fade with age. The flowers are white and are either in large or small panicles. *Buddleja parviflora* is not common in cultivation, and I could not track down a specimen for the Longstock collection. USDA zones 8–9

Buddleja polystachya

The species name is from the Latin *poly*, meaning many, and *stachya*, spike, reference to the many-flowered spikes. It was described and named by Fresen in 1838. Distribution of this species is from East Africa from the uplands regions of Uganda and Kenya north to Somalia, Ethiopia, Eritrea, and Saudi Arabia into Yemen. Its natural habitat is shrubby rocky mountain slopes and open woodland, sometimes beside water sources such as brooks and rivers, at elevations of 700–3600 m (2200–11,800 ft). *Buddleja polystachya* grows as a large shrub or small tree with arching and spreading branches. Young shoots are quadrangular in cross section and covered with greyish white felted hair. Leaves are opposite and when mature measure up to 16 cm (6.5 in) long and 4 cm (1.5 in) across; petioles are 3.3–10 mm (0.13–0.25 in) long. Flowers are sweetly scented and orange, often with a yellow tube; they are borne in dense clusters on terminal inflorescences. Blooms are followed by a dry seed capsule with pale brown seed. The edible fruits are dry orange capsules and are popular among children. During drought years the berries are eaten raw, by both adults and children. *Buddleja polystachya* is not common in cultivation, and I did not manage to get a specimen for the Longstock collection. USDA zones 7–9

Buddleja pterocaulis

The species name is from the Greek *pteron*, meaning wing, and the Latin *caulis*, a stem or stalk. *Buddleja pterocaulis* is an ally of *Buddleja forrestii*, and it was named by A. B. Jackson in 1935. It grows as a large shrub or small tree, to a height of 0.9–5.4 m (3–18 ft) and a spread of 0.9–3.6 m (3–12 ft). *Buddleja pterocaulis* grows at forest edges, mostly along river banks, at elevations of 1800–3600 m (6000–12,000 ft) in China and Burma. The young shoots are covered with light powdery grey hairs. The leaves are opposite, narrow, long, and pointed; they are glabrous once fully expanded. The lilac flowers are borne in terminal panicles, sometimes in the upper leaf axils. This species is not in general cultivation. USDA zone 7

Buddleja pterocaulis var. longifolia

The variety name refers to this plant's relatively long leaves. Our original stock of this variety came from the wonderful woodland hillside Greenways Garden in Devon. The original plant growing out in the garden has very striking foliage, shape and form. The shrub was 2–4 m (6.5–13 ft) in height and spread with soft billowing foliage, the long leaves adding a gentle softness to the overall shape. The National Trust took over the running of the garden in 2002, and they are undoing years of neglect. The garden is rather difficult to get to as you travel for what seems like forever down narrow country lanes. Make sure to book a reservation before your visit, as parking is at a premium. *Buddleja pterocaulis* var. *longifolia* is rare in cultivation. USDA zones 8–9

Buddleja pulchella

The species name is from the Latin *pulchellus*, meaning beautiful and little. It was named and described by N. E. Norman in 1894. This species is distributed throughout South Africa through Zimbabwe and extending into the uplands of Kenya and Tanzania. *Buddleja pulchella* can be found in open mountain forests at elevations of 1200–2000 m (4000–6500 ft). The plant grows to a height of 10 m (32 ft) and has an enormous spread of up to 20 m (65 ft) due to its climbing scrambling habit. The leaves are opposite or subopposite; the petioles are 5–10 mm (0.13–0.25 in) long. The scented flowers are borne in terminal lax open panicles. To some the scent is sweet-smelling, and to others it has an unpleasant after-smell. The flowers are white or pale creamy yellow with orange throats. The blooms are followed by a dry seed capsule, with pale brown seeds. The original plants were introduced into Britain from the Durban Botanic Garden in 1894, but *B. pulchella* is rarely seen in cultivation today. This species eluded my endeavour to add it to the Longstock collection. USDA zones 8–9

Buddleja saligna

Syn. *Chilianthus arboreus*

The species name is derived from the Latin *saligus*, meaning willow-like, in reference to the leaf shape and lax habit. It was named and described by H. B. Willd in 1809. *Buddleja saligna* has a large distribution across South Africa, Natal, Orange Free State, and Transvaal northwards to Zimbabwe. It can be found in mixed scrub, along margins of forests, in coastal thickets, and at the edges of wooded valleys up elevation of 2000 m (6500 ft). In the wild, the plant usually grows as a large shrub to small tree, 7–12 m (23–40 ft) high, although in cultivation it rarely reaches a height of 3 m (10 ft). The bark on mature plants is a creamy brown to dark brown and furrowed longitudinally. Leaves are opposite and narrow. The upper surface is medium to dark green, shiny, and smooth; the under surface is covered with pale stellate hairs. Net veining is conspicuous on the under surface but faint above. Petioles are 2–10 mm (0.08–0.25 in) long. Young shoots are quadrangular in cross section and have four ridges or wings. Flowers are scented (some say like honey), cream or white sometimes with a reddish orange throat, 4 mm (0.16 in) long, and borne from late summer to midwinter. The anthers protrude from the mouth of the flowers, which are arranged in large terminal and auxiliary heads about 12 × 12 cm (4.5 × 4.5 in). Flowers are followed by a small ovoid seed capsule which becomes pale yellowish brown when ripe from early autumn to early spring.

  Buddleja saligna grows easily in a well-drained soil and is resistant to drought. Very little pruning is required—only the occasional shaping. In native medicine a decoction of the leaves is used to relieve coughs and colds. Scrapings of the root are taken as a purgative and to induce vomiting. Modern pharmacology companies are researching the medicinal properties of this species. *Buddleja saligna* is not common in cultivation, but I am very fond of this evergreen and it needs to be promoted. USDA zone 9

Buddleja salviifolia

The species name is made up from the Latin *salve*, meaning well, in good health (sage or *Salvia* is taken as a tonic throughout the Mediterranean region), and *folia*, leaf, and is commonly known as the sage-leafed buddleja. This species was described and named by Lamarck in 1792. *Buddleja salviifolia* has a wide distribution in South Africa in Transvaal, Transkei, Cape

Province, Orange Free State, Lesotho, and Swaziland. Throughout this region it can be found growing on rocky hillsides, at the margins of forests, and along watercourses. The plant is a semi-evergreen small tree or large shrub, multi-stemmed with drooping branches, growing to a height of 4–8 m (13–26 ft). The mature bark is greyish brown and stringy. The young shoots are quadrangular in cross section and covered with reddish brown dense woolly hairs. With age the upper surface turns a dark green to greyish green and becomes wrinkled and puckered. The under surface is covered with rusty to whitish hairs. Apex of the leaf is narrowly tapering, the base is deeply lobed. The leaf has no petiole. The sweetly scented flowers are cream, white, grey, mauve, or purple, sometimes with reddish throat, and 4 mm (0.13 in) long. They are borne in large terminal pyramidal heads measuring about 12 × 12 cm (4.75 × 4.75 in), and the anthers protrude from the mouth of the flower. Sometimes auxiliary heads are present during late summer to midwinter. Seed capsules are ovoid with mid brown seed.

Of all the perfumed buddlejas, many rate *Buddleja salviifolia* to be the finest. Its scent has been described as a strong mignonette to an expensive Chanel perfume. The overall habit of the maturing plant is rather ungainly and is more suited to the larger garden. Plants grow easily in a well-drained soil and are resistant to drought; however, they are prone to insect damage. Prune this species in the spring if required. A decoction made using extracts of the root is used to treat coughs and for the relief of colic, and an infusion of the leaves is applied as an eye lotion. The hard, heavy, pale yellow wood is often used by the Xhosa people for assegais (a short spear) and long straight fishing rods. In the mountains of South Africa *B. salviifolia* is often cultivated for fuel and used as a hedging plant. This species grows easily from cuttings and is common in cultivation. USDA zone 8

Buddleja sphaerocalyx

The species name comes from the Latin word *sphaera*, meaning sphere, and the botanical term *calyx*, the outer whorl of floral leaves. *Buddleja sphaerocalyx* comes from the island of Madagascar, where it can be found growing in the moist mountain forests, often near watercourses, at elevations of 300–2200 m (985–7600 ft). The plant is a vigorous shrub growing to 3 m (10 ft). The young branches are obscurely square, quadrangular in section, leaves opposite without petioles. Flowers are white, borne on auxiliary shoots, sometimes solitary, and often racemose. They are followed by an orange berry containing numerous seeds. I have not had first-hand experience with this species. As far as I am aware, it is rare in cultivation. USDA zones 10–11

Buddleja stenostachya

The species name is from the Greek *steno*, meaning narrowing, and *stachus*, spike or spearlike, in reference to the narrow flower spikes. It was named and described by Rehder and Wilson in 1913. Some taxonomists want to classify this species under *Buddleja crispa*. *Buddleja stenostachya* is native to western Sichuan Province in China. In its natural habitat it grows as a compact deciduous shrub in clearings, by forest edges, and along streams to a height of 3 m (10 ft). The shoots are covered in grey woolly hairs; on the upper surface of the leaves the hairs become sparse with maturity, remaining grey woolly on the under surface. Slender panicles of heliotrope blue flowers are borne in groups of three at the end of the current year's growth. According to the botanical literature, *B. stenostachya* is supposed to be a long-flowering species; however, I found it to be shy to flower—especially when I needed to photograph it. Prune this species in the spring if required. It is not common in cultivation. USDA zones 8–9

Roy Lancaster collected a specimen of *Buddleja stenostachya* (L 1070) above the Tung River at Kangding in western Sichuan. His notes described it as "a large shrub growing to 2 m [6.5 ft] or more growing on steep hill sides." Lancaster added, "in cultivation it becomes a bold shrub to 4 m [13 ft] with grey white downy stems and leaves and long cylindrical inflorescences of small flowers." This plant is grown at the Savill Garden, in Surrey, and the Chelsea Physic Garden, London, and the Sir Harold Hillier Garden and Arboretum may be growing it under the name of *Buddleja nivea*. This form has not yet been introduced to the trade.

Buddleja sterniana

This species' name is from the Latin word *sterno*, meaning to spread. It was described and named by Cotton in 1947. *Buddleja sterniana* is distributed throughout Yunnan Province in China, where it can be found in light scrub, in natural gullies, or by stream edges. The plant is a vigorous deciduous shrub with a rounded, spreading, bushy, and much-branched habit; it reaches a height of 3 m (10 ft). Young shoots are covered with pure white woolly hairs, with maturity becoming sparsely covered in golden brown wool on the upper surface. The opposite leaves are ovate, with heart-shaped bases, and toothed coarsely, often unevenly. The petiole is 2.5 cm (1 in) long. Slender panicles of scented, lavender, orange-eyed flowers up to 3 cm (1.2 in) long are borne in compact narrow clusters on the previous year's growth. The flowers are followed by a dry brown seed capsule.

Buddleja sterniana is only hardy in very sheltered gardens against a warm south-facing wall or in a sunny southern aspect of a woodland garden. Until a plant can be established, I recommend that a spare be grown in a large—25-L (15-in)—pot and brought in for the winter. This species is listed in the *RHS Plant Finder* under the name *Buddleja crispa*. However, I have worked with and examined many plants, as well as done research in the literature, and I am not happy with this suggestion. I feel strongly that this plant is nothing like *Buddleja crispa*. USDA zones 8–9

Buddleja tibetica

The species name refers to this plant's origin in Tibet. *Buddleja tibetica* grows in Tibet in the Himalayas into south-western China, and it is a close ally of *B. farreri*. It is found among scrub, along woodland edges, by natural ditches and ravines, and along stream banks. This deciduous shrub will reach a height of 2 m (6.5 ft). The young shoots and branches are covered with soft white hairs, giving the shoots a felted look; this disappears with age. The older bark is cinnamon brown. The upper surface of leaves is grey felted, disappearing with age; the under surface is white felted, with the majority retained with age. Petioles when present are sometimes winged down the side and up to 5 cm (2 in) long. Flowers are purple when fresh, becoming paler in time. Panicles are produced in midspring on the previous year's growth in clusters up to 20 cm (8 in) long on terminal joints. After the flowers, a small dry seed capsule is formed.

Because flowers come from axils of the previous year's wood, this species should be pruned after flowering. This plant was added to the Longstock collection from a fellow National Council for the Conservation of Plants and Garden Committee member, who had sourced it during his travels in Cornwall. Though a strong grower, I find *Buddleja tibetica* shy to flower. I grow it in a large pot of at least 25 L (15 in) in our hardy ornamental nursery shrub compost and bring it indoors for the winter. Lord Wigram introduced *B. tibetica* into cultivation in 1931 as *Buddleja hastata*. It is listed in the *RHS Plant Finder* under the name *Buddleja crispa*. Based on the plants that I have worked with, read about, and examined, however, I feel strongly that this one is nothing like *B. crispa*. USDA zones 9–10

Buddleja tubiflora

The species name comes from the Latin *tubus*, meaning pipe or tube, and *flora*, the goddess of flowers, in reference to the tubular flowers. The plant was named and described by George Bentham in 1846. *Buddleja tubiflora* has a wide distribution, from Argentina in the south through southern Paraguay spreading over the border of southern Brazil. It is a reasonably vigorous shrub of medium height (2 m, 6.5 ft) and spread (3 m, 10 ft), with a naturally lax floppy habit. The young shoots are covered with a dense reddish brown hair, reducing with age. The orange flowers are 7 × 25 mm (0.25 × 1 in) and borne in axillary clusters along the branch ends; the flowers are all covered with a dense reddish brown hair, also fading with age.

When in flower *Buddleja tubiflora* has a magnetic effect, attracting people to wonder at its amazing flowers. When I showed it in the National Council for the Conservation of Plants and Gardens marquee at Hampton Court, the interest shown by the public caused a major traffic jam. This species can be grown against a warm south-facing wall with some winter protection—the major killer during the winter is rain and wet soil. I grow this plant in a large pot of at least 25 L (15 in) and bring it in for the winter. Very little pruning is required and I tend to prune *B. tubiflora* just to shape. When potting on older specimens, however, a lot of the lateral growth can be pruned back to encourage new growth, which is lovely, thick, and vigorous. Maunder (1984) mentioned that most, if not all, of the stock in Britain originates from a now-lost plant once grown in the Hanbury collection at La Mortola in Italy. This species is one of my top ten favourites. It is not common in cultivation. USDA zones 9–10

Buddleja utahensis

This North American species, named and described by Coville in 1892, grows only in the desert in the Washington region of south-western Utah. It is found at elevations of 800–1525 m (2700–5100 ft) among Joshua tree woodland. *Buddleja utahensis* is a small, compact, dwarf species that grows to a height of 20–30 cm (8–12 in). The small, yellow flowers are borne in clusters of three to seven at the end of short flowering stems. Branches are dense, with semi-deciduous, silver-grey, miniature leaves.

I had difficulty keeping this species alive, even under glass, and I am sure that it was killed with kindness. When I visited the Washington area in Utah, I instantly knew why we had problems. In the wild the plant grows in dry stony ground, with tumbleweeds to keep it company. If I attempted to grow *Buddleja utahensis* again, I would make a compost of crushed house bricks, gravel, and sand with a hint of loam. I would give it a liquid feed every second or third watering, so the feeding is two to four weeks apart. I would overwinter the plant by restricting watering to a minimum once a month or even less. Keep the plant dry by placing a pane of glass over it on wire supports to keep rain or irrigation off the foliage. Plant breeders have not fully exploited the huge potential for this amazing dwarf species. I would like to see some of the better forms of *Buddleja davidii* crossed with *B. utahensis*; such a cross should produce small, compact, free-flowering plants suitable for the smaller garden. (Heaven forbid, it might even lead to one of those ghastly "patio plants.") *Buddleja utahensis* is very rare in cultivation. USDA zone 8

Buddleja venenifera

The species name comes from the Latin *venenifer*, meaning to poison, in reference to the poisonous sap. *Buddleja venenifera* is native to the State of Sonora, Mexico, in the Rio Mayo drainage area of the Sierra Madre Occidental. It was named by T. Makino in 1910, although some authorities classify this species as *Buddleja curviflora*. I disagree, however, because *B. curviflora* comes from the other side of the Pacific Ocean, in Japan. *Buddleja venenifera* can be found along stream and river banks and in forest and other clearings. The shrub resembles a lilac (*Syringa vulgaris*) when in full flower. The lanceolate leaves are medium green above and paler below. Shoots are yellowish grey when young, becoming hairless with age. The lavender purple flower spikes are up to 17.5 cm (7 in) long and are borne from midsummer to early autumn. They are followed by pendulous seed heads in early to late autumn. *Buddleja venenifera* is a difficult species to grow, and it requires glasshouse conditions to be successfully overwintered. This species is classified as a tropical dry forest plant. It requires a very free-draining soil—the crushed brick mix described in chapter 3 would be very good for this species. It is not common in cultivation. USDA zones 8–10

Buddleja venenifera f. *calvescens*

This form's name is from the Latin *calvus*, meaning bald, a reference to the way the plant loses the fine hairs when young. The species is native to Mexico, and the seed of this form was collected in the Ch'ōlli Arboretum by B. Wynn-Jones from Crûg Farm Plants, Gwynedd, Wales, during their South American expedition (specimen B&SWJ 895). The lanceolate leaves differ from the type species in being pale green both above and below. Shoots are yellow-grey when young, becoming hairless with age. The one-sided flower spikes measure 10–30 cm (4–12 in) long, and the blooms are lavender-purple. They are followed by pendulous seed heads from early to late autumn. *Buddleja venenifera* f. *calvescens* is only available through Crûg Farm Plants. USDA zones 8–10

Buddleja verbascifolia

The species name is derived from the genus name *Verbascum* (which is thought to be a corruption of the Latin word *barba*, meaning beard), and *folia*, meaning leaf, in reference to the verbascum-like leaves. *Buddleja verbascifolia* was named and described by Kunth in 1844. The foliage is very rough, and the leaf edges are toothed and wavy. Hairs are present on upper and lower leaf surfaces, thinning with age. Unfortunately, there is little written about this species, so the field notes and overall requirements are lacking.

Buddleja verbascifolia came into the Longstock collection via a keen buddleja fan from France. Though a strong grower, I find this plant to be shy to flower; when it does, it bears off-white flowers in terminal short panicles or cymes. I grow this species in a large pot of at least 25 L (15 in) in our hardy ornamental nursery shrub compost and bring it indoors for the winter. Some authorities classify this species under *Buddleja americana*. *Buddleja verbascifolia* is rare in cultivation. USDA zone 8

Buddleja yunnanensis

The species name refers to this plant's origins in Yunnan Province, China. *Buddleja yunnanensis* was described and named by Gagnepaine in 1912. It is distributed throughout Yunnan Province and south-western China, where it grows at forest edges, in thickets, along mountain stream and river banks, and in natural gullies at elevations of 1000–2500 m (3300–8200 ft).

It is a vigorous shrub, growing to a height of more than 3 m (10 ft). The opposite leaves vary in size from 2 to 12 cm (0.75 to 4.75 in) long by 0.6 to 4.5 cm (0.24 to 1.75 in) wide, sometimes with a short petiole. The lilac flower panicles are borne in terminal spikes, 6 cm (2.4 in) long by 2 cm (0.75 in) wide, sometimes with large leafy bracts.

Though a strong grower, I find *Buddleja yunnanensis* to be shy to flower. I grow it in a large pot of at least 25 L (15 in) in our hardy ornamental nursery stock compost and bring it indoors for the winter. Although I have not seen *B. yunnanensis* in flower, based on its foliage characteristics, I believe that it should be placed with *Buddleja nivea* var. *yunnanensis*; some authorities, however, classify it as *Buddleja stenostachya* var. *yunnanensis*. This species is not listed in the *RHS Plant Finder*, and it is rare in cultivation. USDA zone 8

Plants Often Mistaken for *Buddleja*

Aloysia triphylla

This native of Argentina and Chile is commonly known as lemon or sweet verbena and is a member of the *Verbenaceae*. It grows as a shrub to 3 m (10 ft); the flowers are white, sometimes tinted purple, borne in axillary spikes or terminal panicles. When flowering, *Aloysia triphylla* is sometimes mistaken for a slender *Buddleja*. It is only when the foliage is rubbed and a wonderful lemon scent fills the air that any thought of *Buddleja* disappears.

Cestrum elegans

Syn. *Cestrum purpureum*

This species belongs to the potato family (*Solanaceae*). The plant is a tall, graceful, evergreen, often rambling shrub which grows to 3.5 m (11.5 ft). The stems are covered with soft downy hairs, and the downy leaves resemble those of a buddleja but they are alternate, not opposite as in *Buddleja*. With its clusters of showy red to purple flowers, *C. elegans* is sometimes thought to be *Buddleja colvilei*. *Cestrum elegans* does best when grown against a warm south-facing wall and trained on wires.

Colquhounia

The genus *Colquhounia* is a member of the *Lamiaceae* and comprises three species from the Himalayas. *Colquhounia coccinea* is the only commonly cultivated species and is often mistaken at a distance for a *Buddleja*. The opposite densely white-felted leaves resemble those of *Buddleja davidii*, but the flowers are long, tubular, and nettle-like—quite different. They are scarlet-orange and borne from late summer onwards, until first frosts. The plant is reportedly semi-evergreen in sheltered areas, although in my experience it is deciduous. Every so often *C. coccinea* will suffer terribly with frost damage; however, this plant always breaks from the base and it is root hardy. This species is best grown against a warm south-facing sheltered wall. The variety *Colquhounia coccinea* var. *vestita* grows in dry soils and has a much woollier leaf than the species, although it is less commonly grown.

Phlomis

The genus *Phlomis* is another member of the nettle family, *Lamiaceae*. In their young stages, *Phlomis cashmeriana*, *P. chrysophylla*, *P. italica*, and a few other species are often mistaken for *Buddleja*. The opposite leaves are roughly similar to those of *Buddleja*. The flower structure is very different, however, and is easily distinguished from *Buddleja* by the forward-pointing keel.

Salvia

Salvia, or sages, are members of the *Lamiaceae*. Young plants of many of the shrubby salvias, such as *Salvia sclarea*, resemble a buddleja in their foliage. The flower structure of *Salvia* is very different, however, and is easily distinguished from *Buddleja* by its forward-pointing keel.

Vitex agnus-castus

This species is a member of the *Verbenaceae*. *Vitex agnus-castus* produces terminal racemes of sweetly scented pale violet, bright blue, pale lilac, or white flowers. The foliage is silver-grey, downy, and aromatic. Mature leaves are grey felted beneath, much the same as *Buddleja* 'Lochinch'. When *V. agnus-castus* is in full flower and seen at a distance, it is often mistaken for a dainty free-flowering buddleja. Upon closer inspection, however, the flowers are clearly different from those of *Buddleja* and the leaves have three to seven lobes, and are similar to those of Japanese maples. No buddleja has this leaf form.

Above: 1 *Buddleja* growing along a river at the Sleepy Dragon Nature Reserve in Woolong, China

Right: 2 Millstones hewn from river boulders in natural *Buddleja* habitat in Woolong, China

Below: 3 National Collection of *Buddleja* at Longstock Park Gardens, Hampshire

Right: **4** *Buddleja agathosma*

Below: **5** *Buddleja albiflora*

6 *Buddleja alternifolia*

Left: **7** *Buddleja australis*

Below: **8** *Buddleja caryopteridifolia*

Above: 9 *Buddleja colvilei*   *Below:* 10 *Buddleja cordata*

Above: 11 *Buddleja cordata*   **Below:** 12 *Buddleja coriacea*

13 & 14 *Buddleja crispa*

Right: 15 *Buddleja davidii*

Below: 16 *Buddleja davidii*
var. *magnifica*

Above: **17** *Buddleja davidii* var. *nanhoensis alba*   ***Below:*** **18** *Buddleja fallowiana* var. *alba*

19 *Buddleja indica*   20 *Buddleja japonica*

Above: 22 *Buddleja lindleyana*

Right: 23 *Buddleja loricata*

Left: 21 *Buddleja limitanea*

This page
Top: 24 *Buddleja macrostachya*

Bottom: 25 *Buddleja myriantha*

Opposite
Top: 26 *Buddleja nivea*

Bottom: 27 *Buddleja nivea*
pink-flowered

Above & below: **28 & 29**
Buddleja nivea var. *yunnanensis*

Right: **30** *Buddleja officinalis*

Left: **31** *Buddleja
pterocaulis* var.
longifolia

Below: **32** *Buddleja
saligna*

33 *Buddleja salviifolia*   34 & 35 *Buddleja sterniana*

Left: **36** *Buddleja tibetica*

Below: **37** *Buddleja tubiflora*

Above: **38** *Buddleja tubiflora*

Right: **39** *Buddleja verbascifolia*

40 *Buddleja colvilei* 'Kewensis'

Above: **41** *Buddleja davidii* 'African Queen'   *Below:* **42** *Buddleja davidii* 'Border Beauty'

43 & 44 *Buddleja davidii* 'Dartmoor'

45 *Buddleja davidii* 'Dart's Purple Rain'

46 *Buddleja davidii* 'Dubonnet'

47 *Buddleja davidii* 'Dubonnet'

48 *Buddleja davidii* 'Fascinating'

Above: **49** *Buddleja davidii* 'Glasnevin Hybrid'   *Below:* **50** *Buddleja davidii* 'Golden Sovereign'

Left: 51 *Buddleja davidii* 'Gonglepod'

Below: 52 *Buddleja davidii* 'Harlequin'

Left: **53** *Buddleja davidii* 'Les Kneale'

Below: **54** *Buddleja davidii* 'Nanho Purple'

Right: **55** *Buddleja davidii* 'Opera'

Below: **56** *Buddleja davidii* 'Peace'

Opposite: **61** *Buddleja davidii* 'Southcombe Splendour'

Left: **62** *Buddleja davidii* 'White Ball'

Below left: **63** *Buddleja davidii* 'White Bouquet'

Below: **64** *Buddleja davidii* 'White Cloud'

Opposite
65 & 66 *Buddleja
davidii* 'White Wings'

***Right:* 67** *Buddleja
davidii* 'Widecombe'

***Below:* 68** *Buddleja
'*Lochinch'

Opposite
Top: 69 *Buddleja*
'Pink Delight'

Bottom: 70 *Buddleja*
'West Hill'

This page
Right: 71 *Buddleja*
×*weyeriana* 'Golden Glow'

Below: 72 *Buddleja*
×*weyeriana* 'Honeycomb'

Above left: **73** *Buddleja ×weyeriana* 'Lady de Ramsey'

Above right: **74** *Buddleja ×weyeriana* 'Moonlight'

Left: **75** *Buddleja ×weyeriana* 'Sungold'

Opposite
Top: **76** *Buddleja* 'Wind Tor'

Bottom: **77** *Buddleja* 'Winter Sun'

80 Propagation beds under a polyethylene cover

Left & below: **78 & 79** *Buddleja* bush before and after pruning

81 Peacock butterfly, *Inachis io*

82 White admiral, *Ladoga camilla*

83 Red admiral, *Vanessa atalanta*

Above: **84** Hummingbird hawk-moth, *Macroglossum stellatarum*

85 Silver Y moth, *Autographa gamma*

86 Common wasp, *Vespula vulgaris*

Chapter 2
Hybrids and Cultivars

Buddleja ×alata

This is a naturally occurring hybrid, probably between *Buddleja albiflora* and *B. nivea*. The plant was named and described by Alfred Rehder and E. H. Wilson in 1913. *Buddleja ×alata* has been collected in western Sichuan at elevations of 1300–3000 m (4300–10,000 ft), where it grows as a shrub to 1–3 m (3–10 ft) tall. The flowers are borne from midspring to midautumn in terminal racemes or cymes, as well as in axils of the upper leaves. *Buddleja ×alata* is not common in cultivation. USDA zones 5–8

Buddleja alternifolia 'Argentea'

This cultivar is one of my top ten buddlejas. It has the same growth, flowers, and habit as *Buddleja alternifolia*, but the leaves are covered in silky silvery hairs; the name is from the Latin *argentum*, meaning silver. Like the species, this variety is best shown off by growing it up a single stem to 1.5–2 m (5–6.5 ft), letting its natural arching habit form a graceful weeping free-flowering bush. Place it near to other plants with medium and dark green foliage for that extra contrast. Most good nurseries and garden centres should stock this variety. USDA zone 7–9

Buddleja 'Bicolor'

Syn. *Buddleja davidii* 'Bicolor', *Buddleja ×weyeriana* 'Bicolor'

This plant was raised in 1999 in Athens, Georgia, by Mike Dirr and his team. 'Bicolor' comes from a cross using *Buddleja ×weyeriana* 'Honeycomb' and *B. davidii*. The result has a bicoloured lavender-and-butterscotch flower spike up to 25 cm (10 in) in length. The foliage is greyish green.

Mike tells me that this hybrid was almost thrown out during the selection process. A point to consider when selecting plants—they are not always what they seem, and given a second chance they could exceed all expectations. 'Bicolor' is not yet available in Europe, although it may be purchased through several outlets in the United States. USDA zones 5–9

Buddleja 'Blue Gown'

This hybrid bears blue flowers in mid to late spring. The soft foliage is similar to *Buddleja caryopteridifolia*, and this plant may have resulted from a cross between that species and *Buddleja davidii*. The foliage of *Buddleja* 'Blue Gown' is similar to that of *Buddleja* ×*pikei*. It grows to a height of to 2–3 m (6.5–10 ft) and a spread of 1–2.5 m (3–8 ft).

This plant has a mystery about it. I first came across the name and verbal description of *Buddleja* 'Blue Gown' when Sir John Quicke visited the Longstock collection. He had never seen his specimen in flower and enlisted my advice. When I asked about pruning, he said that all the buddlejas in his collection were pruned early in the spring. I suggested that B. 'Blue Gown' might flower at another time of the year and not to prune this plant for a year or two. Sure enough, late the following spring it was a blaze of colour—much to his delight. Now the plant flowers every spring and only requires very little pruning to keep it in shape; any major pruning is done after flowering. The following summer I visited Sir John Quicke, and he showed me around his beautiful garden at Sherwood, Newton St Cyres, Exeter, Devon. On the same visit I also had the privilege of meeting his head gardener, Vaughan Gallavan. He has started a small commercial nursery at the garden, with Sir John's blessing. The nursery is called Sherwood Cottage Nursery, Newton St Cyres, Exeter. Vaughan intends to stock B. 'Blue Gown' along with some of the other unusual hybrids and plants from the woodland valley garden. This nursery might be the only source of this plant. Sadly, it is not common in cultivation. USDA zones 6–9

Buddleja 'Butterfly Ball'

This hybrid is a deciduous medium-sized shrub. Height can be up to 1–1.5 m (3–5 ft). The grey-green leaves are covered in light grey hairs that fade with age. The white flowers have a golden eye and are arranged in long terminal racemes. Few nurseries stock *Buddleja* 'Butterfly Ball'. USDA zones 5–9

Buddleja 'Clive Farrell'

Syn. *Buddleja davidii* f. *beijing*, *B. davidii* 'Beijing', *B. davidii* 'Clive Farrell'

This late-flowering *Buddleja* was found in Beijing by my friend Clive Farrell. This plant appears similar to *Buddleja davidii*, with lilac-purple flowers in terminal panicles of 9–20 cm (3.5–8 in) long. However, the main flower flush is much later in the season than *Buddleja davidii*: late summer to midautumn or first frosts. Clive, who lives in Dorset and is an expert lepidopterist, planted a 100-m (330-ft) long hedge of this hybrid. It is a real spectacle seen in the late afternoon against an autumn setting sun. Clive has found it very useful for giving the last of the butterflies a top up of nectar for overwintering reserves. This plant is a winner and is on my top ten list of favourite buddlejas. *Buddleja* 'Clive Farrell' is only available at one or two nurseries in the United Kingdom at present, but it is well worth seeking out. The plant has been on one of Clive's web pages for some time now as *B*. 'Clive Farrell'. It has been wrongly listed in the 2004/5 *RHS Plant Finder* as *Buddleja davidii* from Beijing. USDA zones 5–9

Buddleja colvilei 'Kewensis'

The cultivar name is derived from the modern botanical Latin *kewensis*, from Kew. All plants with this name are descended from the original plant that once grew in the temperate house at the Royal Botanic Gardens, Kew. The plant resembles the species in every detail, other than its exceptionally good dark red flowers. Sir Fredrick Stern found it to be hardier when grown in open ground at his garden at Highdown in Sussex, and I have also found this cultivar to be slightly hardier than the species. For best results, protect well from winter winds, avoid winter wind rock, and plant on a free-draining soil. 'Kewensis' was introduced into general cultivation in 1849 and is available at several good nurseries. USDA zones 7–8

Buddleja crispa 'Hulmoon'

This is a new cultivar from the United States. From what I have read and seen of it, I want to buy one now. This shrub has a compact habit, and the flowers are soft pink, similar to *Buddleja crispa*. They are set against wonderful silver-grey foliage, which looks to me as if *B. crispa* has been improved upon. *Buddleja crispa* 'Hulmoon' is not yet in cultivation in Europe. USDA zones 7–9

Buddleja davidii 'Adokeep'

This cultivar was bred and raised by Elizabeth Keep at East Malling Research Station in Kent. *Buddleja davidii* 'Adokeep' is a well-behaved compact bushy small plant that is almost one-third the normal size of *Buddleja davidii*. This plant has been bred for smaller town gardens and containers. The fragrant flowers are deep blue and cover the bush profusely over the summer months to first frost. *Buddleja davidii* 'Adokeep' is available in most major garden centre chains. USDA zones 5–9

Buddleja davidii 'African Queen'

This cultivar was selected in 1959 by the Dutch nurseryman W. Schoemaker from Boskoop. *Buddleja davidii* 'African Queen' is one of the darkest flowered of all the buddlejas. When pruned back and fed in the spring, the plant will grow over 1.8 m (6 ft) high and the same spread across, and the sweetly scented dark panicles can reach 25 cm (10 in) long. The foliage is dark green above and silvery grey beneath. The young shoots are often flushed purple. Some people like the seed heads, as they are flushed purple as well. *Buddleja davidii* 'African Queen' is commonly stocked in many nurseries. USDA zones 5–9

Buddleja davidii 'Amplissima'

This vigorous deciduous shrub grows to 1.5–3 m (5–10 ft). The leaves are dark green, turning bluish green and grey in the summer. Large mauve flower panicles are borne in summer, followed by black berries in autumn. *Buddleja davidii* 'Amplissima' requires full sun and does best in moderate climates. USDA zones 5–9

Buddleja davidii 'Attraction'

This plant was raised in 1999 in Athens, Georgia, by Mr. Mike Dirr and his team. The magenta red flowers are fragrant. The shrub can grow to a height up to 2.75 m (9 ft), with attractive grey-green foliage. The cross comes from the *Buddleja* ×*weyeriana* 'Sungold' stable, but this cultivar is unusual as *B.* ×*weyeriana* 'Sungold' has yellow flowers. *Buddleja davidii* 'Attraction' most closely resembles *Buddleja davidii* 'Royal Red'. Not yet available in Europe, although it is available throughout the United States. USDA zones 5–9

Buddleja davidii 'Bishop's Velvet'

The foliage is dark green above and grey-green below. Young shoots are covered with grey-white hairs that fade with age. The flowers of *Buddleja davidii* 'Bishop's Velvet' are a uniform deep purple, without a coloured throat, and are in typical buddleja terminal panicles. The plant can grow to a height of 2.75 m (9 ft). This is another cultivar I came across when I visited Sir John Quicke's garden. Sherwood Cottage Nursery, Newton St Cyres, Exeter, the new nursery run by his head gardener, might help with sourcing this one. USDA zones 5–9

Buddleja davidii 'Black Knight'

This has to be one of the darkest of all the buddlejas, and the name does it proud. The scented flowers are very dark violet-purple, almost dark grape violet. They are borne on a rather short flower spike compared to other *B. davidii* hybrids and are shown off to the best against plants with silver or gold foliage. The shrub can grow to a height of 4 m (13 ft). *Buddleja davidii* 'Black Knight' is a selection made by Ruy in 1959, and it is rated to be one of the hardiest of all the *B. davidii* hybrids. It won the Royal Horticultural Society's Award of Garden Merit in 1993 and would definitely be on my list of top ten best hybrids. *Buddleja davidii* 'Black Knight' is commonly available at most nurseries. USDA zones 5–9

Buddleja davidii 'Blue Horizon'

The flowers are a good clear blue, and its greyish silver foliage sets off the blooms very well. The branches are naturally arching, and the height can be up to 2.75 m (9 ft). *Buddleja davidii* 'Blue Horizon' is not easy to find in cultivation and is rarely sold in nurseries. USDA zones 5–9

Buddleja davidii 'Bonnie'

This plant was raised in 1999 in Athens, Georgia, by Mike Dirr and his team. Mike named this cultivar after his wife, Bonnie. It is a large vigorous plant growing up to 3 m (10 ft) high and has large greyish green leaves. The flower-heads are 25 cm (10 in) long, pale blue, and sweetly scented. I know that this will be a good hybrid, as Mike has very high standards (especially if he named it after his wife). *Buddleja davidii* 'Bonnie' is not in cultivation in Europe yet, but it can be found in the United States. USDA zones 7–9

Buddleja davidii 'Border Beauty'

This cultivar was selected by Henry Schiphorst from Wageningen, Holland, in 1962. It is an upright, dense, large-leafed shrub that grows to 2 m (6 ft) tall. The young foliage is silver-grey and is nicely set against the clean dark green mature foliage. Flowers are scented and borne in large panicles of rich purple-pink flowers. This is another one of my top ten buddlejas for colour, scent, and overall performance. *Buddleja davidii* 'Border Beauty' is not common in nurseries; however, it is worth the effort to find one. USDA zones 5–9

Buddleja davidii 'Burgundy'

This cultivar is grown by Hines Nursery in Houston, Texas. It looks very similar to *Buddleja davidii* 'Royal Red'. The growth is vigorous and the plant soon becomes a large shrub, growing to a height of 4.5 m (15 ft). The magenta red flowers are scented and borne in panicles up to 32 cm (14 in) long, from midsummer to early autumn. *Buddleja davidii* 'Burgundy' is not available in Europe, but is available through garden centres in the United States. USDA zones 5–9

Buddleja davidii 'Castle School'

This buddleja is early to flower and has fat pale lilac flower spikes that are very fragrant. It resembles *Buddleja* 'Lochinch' but has better colour in both the foliage and flowers. *Buddleja davidii* 'Castle School' is a chance seedling found by nurseryman Martin Hughes-Jones. According to Martin, "It was detected as much by smell as looks. A rather tedious parents evening meeting at Castle School in Tiverton was enlivened by this welcome distraction, and given its perilous position in the cracks in the playground I rescued a piece." It was introduced into commerce in 2004 through his nursery, Sampford Shrubs. They also have an extensive collection of buddleja to view in their Holbrook Garden. USDA zones 5–9

Buddleja davidii 'Charming'

This vigorous cultivar has an upright growth habit which spreads with age. *Buddleja davidii* 'Charming' grows to the height of over 2 m (6.5 ft). During midsummer the scented flowers are borne in lilac, pink, or lavender panicles to 25 cm (10 in) long. This cultivar is available in the United Kingdom and Europe, and may be the same as *Buddleja davidii* 'Pink Charming' widely sold in the United States. USDA zones 7–9

Buddleja davidii 'Cornwall Blue'

This vigorous cultivar grows as a shrub to 1.2–1.8 m (4–6 ft). The deciduous leaves are dark green, turning bluish green and grey in the summer. The fragrant lavender-violet flower panicles are borne from midsummer to early autumn. *Buddleja davidii* 'Cornwall Blue' requires full sun and does best in moderate climates. I would like to tender *Buddleja davidii* 'Trewithen' as a possible parent of this plant. This cultivar is available from several U.S. outlets. USDA zones 5–9

Buddleja davidii 'Croyde'

This is another chance discovery by nurseryman Martin Hughes-Jones, who camps at the village of Croyde in Devon every summer and regularly bicycles throughout the area. He notes that while bicycling through the village "my attention was taken by a conspicuous buddleja on a piece of waste ground. The flower spikes were purple, slender, and very long and rather fine." So a small piece found its way into his pannier bags. The foliage is long and narrow, similar to that of *Buddleja nanhoensis*, and is greyish olive green. *Buddleja davidii* 'Croyde' was introduced into commerce in 2004 through Sampford Shrubs; they also have an extensive collection of buddleja to view in their Holbrook Garden. USDA zones 5–9

Buddleja davidii 'Darkness'

The foliage is deciduous; leaves are dark green, bluish green and grey in the summer. The plant has a wide-spreading arching habit and grows relatively quickly to 1.5–3 m (5–10 ft) tall. Deep blue to purple flowers are borne in summer, followed by black berries in autumn. *Buddleja davidii* 'Darkness' does best in full sun and in moderate climates. Not in cultivation in Europe, although it is available in the United States. USDA zones 5–9

Buddleja davidii 'Dartmoor'

This hybrid was found on Dartmoor near Yelverton Devon in 1971 by Mr. Hayles, a retired gardener from the United States. He was walking with his wife when he spied an unusual buddleja growing and flowering on the edge of a ravine. With his wife clinging onto him, Hayles managed to reach down to the plant long enough to collect some propagation material. *Buddleja davidii* 'Dartmoor' was released into commerce during 1973.

In flower, *B. davidii* 'Dartmoor' is one of the easiest to identify by the size and shape of the flower-heads. The rich lilac flowers are unique, as they are borne on large branched racemes, whereas other cultivars have single, unbranched terminal inflorescences. This plant will grow to a mature height of 5 m (16 ft), but it responds well to hard pruning. It has proved to root easily from softwood cuttings. The shrub is hardy to –15°C (5°F) and root hardy in colder climates. I would place this on my list of top ten hybrids. It received the Royal Horticultural Society's Award of Garden Merit in 1993. *Buddleja davidii* 'Dartmoor' is easily found at garden centres and is common in cultivation. USDA zones 5–9

Buddleja davidii 'Dart's Ornamental White'

This is a cultivar introduced from the Dart's Nursery in the Netherlands. It looks similar to several other white-flowered forms, and I cannot find a single identifiable feature that sets it apart from *Buddleja davidii* var. *alba*. I am sure that others might find one. *Buddleja davidii* 'Dart's Ornamental White' is not commonly sold in nurseries. USDA zones 5–9

Buddleja davidii 'Dart's Papillion Blue'

This is another introduction from the Dart's Nursery. The habit is open and lax, and the foliage is dark green. I cannot find a single identifiable characteristic that sets it aside from *Buddleja davidii*. *Buddleja davidii* 'Dart's Papillion Blue' is not commonly found in nurseries. USDA zones 5–9

Buddleja davidii 'Dart's Purple Rain'

I purchased 'Dart's Purple Rain' from a small nursery in Essex. The owner was a landscape designer keen on using buddlejas in his planting schemes; he longed for a new cultivar that cast its old seed heads while keeping the overall look neat and tidy. *Buddleja davidii* 'Dart's Purple Rain' seldom sets seed heads, and this was his selection. After a spring pruning, the plant's deep purple flower spikes will grow up to 2–2.5 m (6.5–8 ft). At the time of writing this cultivar is no longer listed in the *RHS Plant Finder*; however, it is part of the Longstock collection. USDA zones 6–9

Buddleja davidii 'Deep Lavender'

The staff of Carroll Gardens, Westminster, Maryland, found this butterfly bush, without a name, in an old nursery. *Buddleja davidii* 'Deep Lavender' is a profuse bloomer. It has wide flower trusses of deep lavender-lilac with pronounced orange eyes. Each floret is heavily ruffled and fringed. The plant reaches a height of 2.4 m (8 ft). This hybrid does best in full sun. It is not in cultivation in Europe but is available through a few outlets in the United States. USDA zones 5–9

Buddleja davidii 'Dubonnet'

This hybrid grows as an upright shrub to a height over 2 m (6.5 ft). During midsummer it bears deep purple flowers with light orange throat rings and eyes. *Buddleja davidii* 'Dubonnet' is very popular, and it has been around for some time. Although this is a good plant, it is available at few nurseries. USDA zones 5–9

Buddleja davidii 'Ecolonia'

This semi-evergreen dwarf shrub reaches a height of 0.9–1.2 m (3–4 ft). The flowers are mauve-blue and borne in mid to late summer. The foliage is silvery. *Buddleja davidii* 'Ecolonia' is not yet widely available in the United Kingdom. USDA zones 5–9

Buddleja davidii 'Ellen's Blue'

This relatively new cultivar started life as a stray seedling from *Buddleja* 'Lochinch' in Ellen Hornig's garden in New York. This compact buddleja only grows to 1.25 m (4 ft) height and is smothered with terminal spikes of unique blue-violet flowers which attract butterflies from miles around. The dwarf and the prolific-flowering hybrids are making a big impact throughout the American and European horticultural trades. Heronswood Nursery in Kingston, Washington, is the licence holder for *Buddleja davidii* 'Ellen's Blue'. This plant has not yet reached the commercial market in Europe; however, I was kindly given one for the Longstock collection by Bernheim Arboretum. USDA zones 6–9

Buddleja davidii 'Empire Blue'

This is an older cultivar with an upright habit that grows to 2.75 m (8 ft). It bears strong lavender, almost blue, flowers with orange eyes in small spikes that have a lovely fragrance. Due to the small size of the flower spikes, many new cultivars outperform *Buddleja davidii* 'Empire Blue', but none comes close to it for the colour of the flowers. It has been in cultivation since 1941 and was given the Royal Horticultural Society's Award of Garden Merit in 1993. This hybrid is sold by many nurseries. USDA zones 5–9

Buddleja davidii 'Fascinating'

I came across this cultivar in an out-of-the-way nursery in Guernsey. I took several cuttings and left the donor plant in my friend's garden, where it still lives. The cuttings all rooted to form strong, healthy, upright plants to 2.5 m (8 ft) tall, with scented, deep purple-blue flower spikes. The foliage is clean dark green and contrasts well with the upright flowers. Bean (1950) listed this hybrid as the same as *Buddleja davidii* 'Fascination'; however, the plant in the Longstock collection is totally different from his description of "full panicles of vivid pink." *Buddleja davidii* 'Fascinating' is not common in cultivation and is difficult to find in the nursery trade. USDA zones 5–9

Buddleja davidii 'Fascination'

This American hybrid was selected by Paul Schmidt of Youngstown, Ohio, in 1940. When pruned early in the spring and fed well, *Buddleja davidii* 'Fascination' is a vigorous grower of good habit, attaining a height and spread up to 2.1 m (7 ft). The foliage is silvery grey beneath; leaves are dark green above when mature and silvery when young. The broad panicles of rich lilac-pink flowers are lightly scented. USDA zones 7–9

Buddleja davidii 'Flaming Violet'

The fragrant, violet-purple flower spikes of this cultivar are 20 cm (8 in) long. The foliage has a clean dark green look about it, making this buddleja a wonderful shrub. *Buddleja davidii* 'Flaming Violet' is not common in nurseries or cultivation, however, and I do think that it needs to be promoted more. USDA zones 6–9

Buddleja davidii 'Fortune'

This is a vigorous shrub growing to a height of 2.5 m (8 ft), with a rounded habit. The flowers are a medium purple, each with a yellow to orange eye; they are produced in very long panicles reaching 40 cm (16 in). *Buddleja davidii* 'Fortune' strongly resembles *Buddleja davidii* var. *magnifica*, especially the colour and length of the flower spike. When it comes to size and quantity of flower, *Buddleja davidii* 'Fortune' is a wonderful plant. It is an old cultivar introduced into cultivation in 1936. It is not common in cultivation but well worth tracking down if the flower size appeals. USDA zones 5–9

Buddleja davidii 'Glasnevin Hybrid'

Syn. *Buddleja davidii* 'Glasnevin', *Buddleja davidii* 'Glasnevin Blue'

This hybrid was named by the Earl of Stair in Lochinch, Scotland, after Glasnevin Garden, a wonderful garden in Ireland. It resulted from a cross between *Buddleja fallowiana* and *B. davidii*, the same parents used in the production of *Buddleja* 'Lochinch' and *B. davidii* 'West Hill'. *Buddleja davidii* 'Glasnevin Hybrid' is a strong-growing shrub with good qualities from both parents, and it is hardier than *B. fallowiana*. It has lovely dusty light blue flowers. The leaves are covered with white felted hairs on the under surface. USDA zones 7–8

Buddleja davidii 'Golden Sovereign'

Peter G. Addison introduced this selection in 1991. He came across it as a sport of *Buddleja davidii* 'Empire Blue' in his nursery. The leaves have an overall golden colour, which is brightest in a sunny situation. This lax shrub grows to a height of 1.5–3 m (5–10 ft) and produces blue flowers. *Buddleja davidii* 'Golden Sovereign' is not common in cultivation. USDA zones 6–9

Buddleja davidii 'Gonglepod'

The name "gonglepod" is a nonsense word used around the English nursery where this plant appeared as a chance seedling. *Buddleja davidii* 'Gonglepod' bears long, narrow, blue-mauve flower spikes in mid to late summer. The flowers are scented and produced on arching branches set against grey-green foliage. This selection has a spreading habit and grows to a height of 1.2–1.5 m (4–5 ft). It is not common in cultivation. USDA zones 5–9

Buddleja davidii 'Guinevere'

This is one of the darkest of all the buddlejas, and the closest to it is *Buddleja davidii* 'Black Knight'. The nearly black-purple flowers are borne from late spring to early summer. The foliage is dark blue-green, large, and lustrous. *Buddleja davidii* 'Guinevere' is a robust grower, attaining a height of 3 m (10 ft). This cultivar was originally rejected during the selection process. A student of Mike Dirr, Cindy Burkes, saw its true potential and rescued it from the bonfire heap. She grew it on, and Dirr eventually introduced it to the trade. Plants are not yet available in Europe, although they may be purchased from several outlets in the United States. USDA zones 6–9

Buddleja davidii 'Harlequin'

This plant arose as a sport of *Buddleja davidii* 'Royal Red' and has been in cultivation since 1964. The leaves have a creamy yellow-white margin, and the plant looks good even when not in flower. *Buddleja davidii* 'Harlequin' is notorious for throwing nonvariegated shoots, and these should be dealt with right away. If growth is young and soft, the best way to remove it is by rubbing it off the main stem. If the reverted shoot is cut off with a pair of secateurs, small dormant buds in the shoot axils will develop and other shoots will multiply and grow. In the United States *B. davidii* 'Harlequin' is prone to attack by mites, and a lot of U.S. nurseries have stopped propagating, growing, stocking, and selling this cultivar due to its attraction for mites. When grown well—without pests and reversion—the combination of this plant's flower and leaf colours is striking. This cultivar is commonly available at garden centres and nurseries. USDA zones 7–9

Buddleja davidii 'Ile de France'

The leaves of *Buddleja davidii* 'Ile de France' are 20 cm (8 in) long and deep green. The fragrant flowers are rich violet-purple and borne in large inflorescences, up to 0.6 m (2 ft) in length, from midsummer to midautumn. The seed heads are long and gracefully arching. When established and pruned back every spring, this cultivar reaches a height of 2.4 m (8 ft). The growth habit is upright, dense, slightly open, and arching. A. Nonin of Chatillion-sous-Bagneux, France, introduced this selection around 1930; the parents were *Buddleja davidii* var. *magnifica* and *B. davidii* var. *veitchiana*. *Buddleja davidii* 'Ile de France' is not easy to find, but the effort is well worth it and specialist nurseries do stock it. USDA zones 5–9

Buddleja davidii 'Les Kneale'

The pinkish flowers are borne in long weeping panicles. This hybrid has striking foliage with a golden yellow quality about it. When it is in a mixed border, such as the Longstock collection, *Buddleja davidii* 'Les Kneale' stands out as being something different. You will either love this plant for its foliage or you will take an instant dislike to it. I love it because of the fresh yellow-grey colour of the shoots and leaves. This hybrid is not easy to find but well worth the effort to track down. USDA zones 7–9

Buddleja davidii 'Malvern Blue'

The foliage is narrow, dark green above, and grey-green below. The flowers are a deep purple-blue with pale bluish white eyes and orange throats, borne in terminal panicles. This is another hybrid I came across when I visited Sir John Quicke's garden. He had bought it at Southcombe Nursery, Kewton, Exeter, Devon. Sherwood Cottage Nursery, Newton St Cyres, Exeter, the new nursery run by Quicke's head gardener, might be helping to distribute this cultivar. USDA zones 5–9

Buddleja davidii Masquerade ('Notbud')

This cultivar was bred and raised by the East Malling Research Station; Notcutt's Nurseries of Suffolk are the license holders. The plant is an upright shrub that grows to a height of 2.4 m (8 ft). It produces large panicles of scented, purple-red flowers. The leaves have a broad, irregular, bright cream and yellow variegation. Many garden centres stock Masquerade. USDA zones 6–9

Buddleja davidii 'Miss Ellen'

This plant is compact, has an outstanding quality of robust blue-green foliage, and looks good throughout the summer and well into the autumn—even in Georgia's hot summers. The fragrant, vibrant dark blue flowers have orange eyes and are borne in panicles up to 25 cm (10 in) long. This promising new hybrid was raised and introduced by Steve Thomas of Greene Hill Nursery in Georgia, U.S.A. *Buddleja davidii* 'Miss Ellen' is not available on the European market yet. USDA zones 5–9

Buddleja davidii 'Mongo'

This cultivar was introduced by the wholesaler Monrovia Nursery, U.S.A., in 1984. *Buddleja davidii* 'Mongo' is a deciduous shrub with an open habit; it has slender, arching branches and can reach 1.75–2 m (5.8–6.6 ft). The fragrant, pale lavender terminal flower spike is 10–18 cm (4–7 in) long. This hybrid has an extended flowering season lasting from midsummer to early autumn. *Buddleja davidii* 'Mongo' is not yet available in European nurseries. For a list of U.S. retail outlets, see www.monrovia.com. USDA zones 5–6

Buddleja davidii 'Moonshadow'

This is a new compact low-growing buddleja from the United States. One of the parents is *Buddleja davidii* 'Nanho Purple'. The blooms change colour from lilac-purple in bud to soft lavender flowers. During hot weather the flowers are nearly white and they look spectacular in moonlight. The narrow leaves are dark bluish green. The branches spread to 1.25 m (4 ft), and the plant reaches a height of 1 m (3 ft). The changing flowers set against the dark foliage and the compact habit should make this a winner in the near future. *Buddleja davidii* 'Moonshadow' is not yet available on the European market, but it is available in the U.S. retail trade. USDA zones 5–9

Buddleja davidii 'Nanho Blue'

Syn. *Buddleja davidii* 'Nanho Petite Indigo', *Buddleja davidii* 'Petite Indigo'

Bred in Holland, this hybrid is closely related to *Buddleja davidii* var. *nanhoensis*, with indigo flowers and a similar habit, and it has *Buddleja davidii* 'Royal Red' in its parentage. *Buddleja davidii* 'Nanho Blue' is a dainty plant, which looks good in a multiple odd-numbered planting. If unchecked, it will grow to 1.5 m (4 ft). The plants flower much better if pruned in the spring, producing flower spikes of 15 cm (6 in) long. This hybrid was given the Royal Horticultural Society's Award of Garden Merit in 1993. Many nurseries grow and stock this plant. USDA zones 5–9

Buddleja davidii 'Nanho Purple'

Syn. *Buddleja davidii* 'Nanho Petite Purple'

This Dutch selection is closely related to *B. davidii* var. *nanhoensis*, with rich lavender-purple flowers and a similar habit, and it has *Buddleja davidii* 'Royal Red' in its parentage. *Buddleja davidii* 'Nanho Purple' is a deciduous shrub with an arching, spreading habit which typically grows to 0.9–1.5 m (3–5 ft) tall if not cut back in late winter and 0.6–0.9 m (2–3 ft) tall if cut back. The spike-shaped terminal clusters of rich lavender-purple flowers, to 15 cm (6 in) long, bloom from early summer to early autumn and sometimes to first frost. In USDA zones 5 and 6, this plant will often die to the ground in winter and therefore is often grown in the manner of an herbaceous perennial. Even if plants do not die to the ground in winter, they usually grow more vigorously, produce superior flowers, and maintain a better shape if cut to the ground in late winter each year. *Buddleja davidii* 'Nanho Purple' has been in cultivation since 1980, and it was given the Royal Horticultural Society's Award of Garden Merit in 2002. The plant is grown by many nurseries and should be easy to track down. USDA zones 5–9

Buddleja davidii 'Niche's Choice'

This cultivar was raised and introduced into cultivation by Niche Gardens of Chapel Hill, North Carolina, U.S.A. The arching branches are 1.2–1.5 m (4–5 ft) long. If cut back each spring, the branches carry purple-pink flower spikes up to 25 cm (10 in) long from early summer to early autumn. The foliage is a fresh green and sets off the flowers well. *Buddleja davidii* 'Niche's Choice' is not yet available in the European market. USDA zones 5–9

Buddleja davidii 'Opera'

This cultivar grows to a height of 1.8 m (6 ft). It has a dense bushy habit and is usually chosen and grown for its long, scented, bright fuchsia-pink flower spikes. *Buddleja davidii* 'Opera' is a reliable pink; I would rate it third or fourth after *B.* 'Pink Delight' and *B. davidii* 'Border Beauty'. USDA zones 7–9

Buddleja davidii 'Orchid'

This is distributed by Niche Gardens, Chapel Hill, North Carolina, U.S.A.; they originally sourced it from Anne Rainey of Columbia, South Carolina. It is a dense, compact shrub with slender, arching branches in every direction; the branches are flushed red in autumn. The overall shape is very good and is retained throughout the year. The leaves are narrow, veined dark green above, and silvery grey beneath. The lavender to pale purple flower spikes are fragrant. I have not yet found a supplier for *Buddleja davidii* 'Orchid' in the United Kingdom or Europe. USDA zones 5–9

Buddleja davidii 'Orchid Beauty'

This plant has a rounded habit, reaching a height and spread of 1.2 m (4 ft). *Buddleja davidii* 'Orchid Beauty' is beautiful with long clear lavender-pink panicles of sweetly scented flowers, a combination which is distinctive from all other buddlejas. The young foliage is white, becoming dark green above and silvery white below with age. To me this cultivar is almost as good as *Buddleja davidii* 'Border Beauty', but the foliage lacks the contrast. *Buddleja davidii* 'Orchid Beauty' is not widely available, although a few specialist nurseries sell it. USDA zones 7–9

Buddleja davidii 'Peace'

This plant was introduced into cultivation in late 1945 to commemorate the end of World War II. *Buddleja davidii* 'Peace' is a good vigorous plant. Some say it resembles a vigorous form of *Buddleja davidii* 'White Ball', and it is often considered to be the best white *B. davidii*. The plant can grow to 2 m (6.5 ft) or more in one year. Its overall habit is upright, round, and dense. Leaves are long and narrow, light green to grey-green, and arranged densely along the stem. The white blooms are up to 25–30 cm (10–12 in) long, borne in panicles poised upright over the main foliage mass; the individual flowers have pronounced orange throats. The flower spikes soon fade to brown, however, and become unsightly—a problem with most of the white-flowered forms. Deadheading is strongly recommended to keep the plant looking good. Because this is one of the oldest and hardiest white cultivars of *B. davidii*, it should not be difficult to track down. USDA zones 5–9

Buddleja davidii Peacock **('Peakeep')**

This cultivar was bred and raised by Elizabeth Keep at East Malling Research Station in Kent. Peacock is a compact bushy plant, growing to 0.9–1.5 m (3–5 ft), almost one-third the normal size of most *B. davidii* cultivars. The pink flowers are fragrant and cover the bush profusely over the summer months right to first frost. This has been bred for smaller town gardens and containers. Most large garden centres stock this hybrid. USDA zones 6–9

Buddleja davidii 'Petite Plum'

Syn. *Buddleja davidii nanhoensis* 'Monum', *B. davidii* 'Nanho Petite Plum', *B. davidii nanhoensis* 'Petite Plum'

This cultivar was introduced in 1984 by Monrovia Nursery in the United States; the name, however, has been changed several times. *Buddleja davidii* 'Petite Plum' is a compact deciduous shrub with arching branches; it can reach a height of 1.75–2 m (5.8–6.6 ft). The fragrant dark lavender to reddish purple flowers are borne on a terminal spike measuring 10–25 cm (4–10 in) long. This cultivar was raised with an extended flowering season and the smaller garden in mind, and it is available at garden centres throughout the United States. I note that the 2004/5 *RHS Plant Finder* gives 'Petite Plum' as a synonym for 'Nanho Purple'. USDA zones 5–9

Buddleja davidii 'Petite Snow'

Syn. *Buddleja davidii* 'Monite'

Monrovia Nursery introduced this cultivar in 1984. It is a compact deciduous shrub with arching branches and medium green leaves with a silvery cast. The plant can reach a height of 1.25–1.75 m (4.2–5.8 ft). It bears terminal spikes of fragrant white flowers, 25–30 cm (10–12 in) long. This hybrid was raised with an extended flowering season and smaller gardens in mind. In recent U.S. trials, *Buddleja davidii* 'Petite Snow' was voted as the best white-flowered buddleja. USDA zones 5–9

Buddleja davidii 'Pink Pearl'

This old European hybrid is no longer common in cultivation. The plant has an upright dense habit and grows to a height of 1.5–2.4 m (5–8 ft). The pale lilac to pink flowers have soft yellow eyes and are arranged in long dense panicles. The foliage is a grey-green. It will be difficult to source young plants of *Buddleja davidii* 'Pink Pearl'. USDA zones 6–9

Buddleja davidii 'Pink Spreader'

Another Dutch cultivar, *Buddleja davidii* 'Pink Spreader', as the name suggests, has a wider spread (1.5–2.4 m, 5–8 ft) than height (1.2–1.8 m, 4–6 ft). Its greyish green foliage nicely sets off the pink flower spikes, which measure 7.5–25 cm (3–10 in). *Buddleja davidii* 'Pink Spreader' is useful set in the middle of a mixed low-maintenance border. It is not easy to source; however, I did find one for the Longstock collection. The plant I sourced came from an amazing nursery, Baumschulen Peter Zwingingberg Jr. in Boskoop, Holland. It took me over three hours of careful looking through just one-quarter of his 0.8-ha (2-acre) nursery. This place is the horticultural equivalent of Aladdin's cave, Mecca, and Shangri La all rolled into one. I was just like a child in a sweet shop. Peter stocks a vast array of rare and unusual plants. USDA zones 5–9

Buddleja davidii 'Pixie Blue'

This looks as if it has *Buddleja davidii* var. *nanhoensis* in its parentage. *Buddleja davidii* 'Pixie Blue' is a dwarf shrub of rounded habit. The narrow fresh green leaves make a good setting for the deep blue flowers, which are borne in long terminal panicles and appear in midsummer. 'Pixie Blue' is in general cultivation and should not be difficult to source from specialist nurseries. USDA zones 5–9

Buddleja davidii 'Pixie Red'

This cultivar resembles *Buddleja davidii* 'Royal Red' in flower colour, with the slender foliage, size, and shape of *Buddleja davidii* var. *nanhoensis*. *Buddleja davidii* 'Pixie Red' is a dwarf shrub of rounded habit. The narrow fresh green leaves provide a good setting for the red flowers, which are borne in long terminal panicles and appear during midsummer. 'Pixie Red' is in general cultivation and should not be difficult to source from specialist nurseries. USDA zones 5–9

Buddleja davidii 'Pixie White'

Overall this is a dwarf shrub of rounded habit; its narrow fresh green leaves make a good foil for the white flowers. The flowers are produced in long terminal panicles and appear during midsummer. This looks as if it has *Buddleja davidii* var. *nanhoensis* in its parentage. *Buddleja davidii* 'Pixie White' is in general cultivation and should be available at specialist nurseries. USDA zones 5–9

Buddleja davidii 'Potter's Purple'

Jack Potter of Wister Garden in Swarthmore, Pennsylvania, introduced this selection in 1984. Generally speaking, *Buddleja davidii* 'Potter's Purple' is rather coarse and irregular in habit. Early in the season the branches are stiff, giving it an upright shape; with maturity, however, the branches arch and spread, giving it the overall shape of a vase. The flowers open in early summer, reach full bloom by midsummer, and continue until early autumn. The flowers are not strongly perfumed. The large thick flower spikes range from vibrant violet to dark purple to glowing purple; they are set against handsome large dark leaves with a silvery underside. Although hard to find, this buddleja is worth looking for if you want a dark alternative to *Buddleja davidii* 'African Queen' or *B. davidii* 'Black Knight'. At present *B. davidii* 'Potter's Purple' is not available in the European market, although it is sold in the United States. USDA zones 6–9

Buddleja davidii 'Princeton Purple'

The blue-purple flowers of this hybrid are produced in broad cone-shaped panicles. The panicles are wider than those of most buddlejas in cultivation, but not as broad as those of *B. davidii* 'Dartmoor'. *Buddleja davidii* 'Princeton Purple' resembles *Buddleja davidii* 'Dubonnet'. The leaves are dense, of a rough texture, and thicker than most *B. davidii* hybrids. The plant will grow to a height of 2 m (6.5 ft) after heavy spring pruning. *Buddleja davidii* 'Princeton Purple' is not common in cultivation and it is difficult to find young stock. USDA zones 6–9

Buddleja davidii Purple Emperor ('Pyrkeep')

This hybrid was bred and raised by Elizabeth Keep at East Malling Research Station in Kent. Purple Emperor is a compact bushy plant that reaches 1.2 m (4 ft), almost one-third the normal size of *Buddleja davidii*. The large, fragrant flowers are mauve purple and cover the bush profusely over the summer months to first frost. This plant was bred for smaller gardens and containers. *Buddleja davidii* Purple Emperor ('Pyrkeep') is available at garden centres. USDA zones 5–9

Buddleja davidii 'Purple Friend'

Andrew Bullock at The Lavender Garden, Tetbury, Gloucestershire raised this hybrid and introduced it in 2002. This small shrub grows to 1.2 m (4 ft), with grey-green foliage. The deep purple flower spike is almost as dark as *Buddleja davidii* 'Black Knight'. *Buddleja davidii* 'Purple Friend' is a typical *B. davidii* cultivar and is fully hardy in free-draining soil. USDA zones 5–9

Buddleja davidii 'Purple Prince'

One of the oldest *Buddleja* hybrids, this cultivar is also one of the most visited by butterflies. *Buddleja davidii* 'Purple Prince' was selected by Paul Schmidt of Youngstown, Ohio, and introduced to the U.K. by Veitch through his nursery in England in 1945. It is believed to have *B. davidii* 'Ile de France' in its parentage. The plant is a vigorous upright shrub up to 3 m (10 ft). It produces very fragrant, deep violet to light purple flowers with golden eyes. The general habit of the plant is messy, however, opening out in the centre with age. In addition, the flower spike is narrow compared to better, more compact hybrids. *Buddleja davidii* 'Purple Prince' is not common in European nurseries. USDA zones 6–9

Buddleja davidii 'Raspberry Wine'

A new introduction promising to have a great future in the nursery trade, *Buddleja davidii* 'Raspberry Wine' originated from Carroll Gardens in Westminster, Maryland. It has unique flower colour and shape. The large and very fragrant flowers are a deep mauve rose with golden eyes. This cultivar's name is quite apt, as the flowers look like raspberry wine. Mike Dirr, however, reports that it is similar to *Buddleja davidii* 'Summer Rose'. USDA zones 6–9

Buddleja davidii 'Red Plume'

This is a vigorous hybrid reaching over 3 m (10 ft), with a spread of 3.5 m (12 ft). Flowers are a rich velvety reddish violet, resembling *Buddleja davidii* 'Royal Red'. Sadly, there are no nurseries in Europe listing it for sale, although it is available in the United States. USDA zones 6–9

Buddleja davidii 'Rice Creek'

Betty Ann Addison and Harvey Buchite of Rice Creek Gardens introduced this selection. It is an upright shrub that grows to a height of 1.5–3 m (5–10 ft) and it bears purple flowers throughout the summer. So far it has proved to be hardier than most lavender-flowered cultivars, and it is reported to be root hardy in Minnesota. *Buddleja davidii* 'Rice Creek' is not yet available in Europe, but it can be purchased from Rice Creek Gardens and garden centres in the United States. USDA zones 6–9

Buddleja davidii 'Royal Purple'

This is a vigorous shrub reaching a height of 4–5 m (13–16 ft). In midsummer, the purple flowers are borne in terminal panicles measuring 15–23 cm (6–9 in). *Buddleja davidii* 'Royal Purple' is not easy to find in the nursery trade. USDA zones 6–9

Buddleja davidii 'Royal Red'

One of the best red-flowered buddlejas, *Buddleja davidii* 'Royal Red' comes closest to pure red. The rich magenta-red flowers are borne on spiked panicles up to 35 cm (14 in) long from midsummer to early autumn. If unchecked, the plant can grow to a height of 4.5 m (15 ft); it then becomes unsightly as it opens out, splaying and spreading with age. It responds well to hard pruning in the spring after frosts. In USDA zone 5 it is root hardy, growing like a hardy herbaceous perennial and being cut down every winter. *Buddleja davidii* 'Royal Red' has been in cultivation since 1941, and the Royal Horticultural Society gave it an Award of Garden Merit in 1993. USDA zones 5–9

Buddleja davidii 'Royal Red Variegata'

This cultivar arose as a sport of *Buddleja davidii* 'Royal Red'. To me, the rich crimson-purple is one of the best colours among the red-flowered buddlejas. The flower panicles, borne from midsummer to early autumn, are up to 30 cm (12 in) long. The green leaves have creamy white margins, setting off the dark red flowers beautifully. As with many variegated plants, however, look out for reversion. *Buddleja davidii* 'Royal Red Variegata' tends to throw vigorous green shoots and, if these are not removed promptly, loses the variegation, similar to *B. davidii* Masquerade ('Notbud'). In 1993 I came across this cultivar by chance at Mill Race Nursery in Essex, and since then I have not found another supplier. USDA zones 8–9

Buddleja davidii 'Salicifolia'

This cultivar's name is derived from the Latin *salix*, meaning willow, and *folia*, leaf, in reference to the long narrow leaves. *Buddleja davidii* 'Salicifolia' is an unusual form and it makes an interesting shrub when mature; however, it can look very sparse while it is establishing. The foliage is beautifully set off against the wonderful *Buddleja davidii* blue-lilac flower spikes. I have found only one nursery supplying this plant: Eildon Plants of Melrose, Scotland. USDA zones 6–9

Buddleja davidii 'Santana'

Syn. *Buddleja davidii* 'Sultan', *B. davidii* 'Sultana'

A relatively new variegated form of *Buddleja davidii*, this cultivar has very showy soft, narrow leaves that are broadly and irregularly edged with golden yellow. The reddish purple flowers are borne from midsummer to early autumn. I found this plant difficult to establish during our normal wet British summers; however, during the summer of 2003 it produced an abundance of strong growth. Owing to the poor growth and difficulty in getting this plant established, *Buddleja davidii* 'Santana' has not had a good start in the trade. There are several nurseries listed in the *RHS Plant Finder* that stock it. USDA zones 7–9

Buddleja davidii 'Snowbank'

This is another American cultivar with pure white flowers. The shrub grows to 1.8–2.4 m (6–8 ft) tall and 1.2–1.8 m (4–6 ft) wide. The fragrant white flowers are borne in terminal panicles to 15 cm (6 in) long, from midsummer to early autumn. *Buddleja davidii* 'Snowbank' is not yet available in the European market, but it can be found in the United States. USDA zones 5–9

Buddleja davidii 'Southcombe Blue'

Trevor Wood selected this seedling at Southcombe Garden, Devon, in the 1970s. The plant has an open semi-lax habit and reaches 1.8–2.4 m (6–8 ft) in height. The foliage is dark green above and olive green below. The flowers are a light violet-blue; Trevor reports they are bluer than in many cultivars. *Buddleja davidii* 'Southcombe Blue' is commonly available in Europe. USDA zones 5–9

Buddleja davidii 'Southcombe Splendour'

This is another cultivar selected by Trevor Wood at Southcombe Garden. The plant has an open semi-lax habit and grows to 1.5–2.1 m (5–7 ft). One of the main features of *Buddleja davidii* 'Southcombe Splendour' is the main flower spikes have small spikes protruding from them. The large dense flowers are light violet-blue and held upright high above the foliage. The leaves are pale grey with a pale golden hue to the upper growths. This cultivar is available through several nurseries in the United Kingdom. USDA zones 6–9

Buddleja davidii 'Strawberry Lemonade'

Syn. *Buddleja davidii* 'Monrell', *B. davidii* 'Monrel'

This is a new hybrid bred in the United States by Monrovia Nursery. *Buddleja davidii* 'Strawberry Lemonade' is a variegated shrub with distinctive pure white leaf edges. It appears to be a very good foliage plant. The clear soft pink flowers are borne in midsummer. It is available at garden centres throughout the United States. USDA zones 6–9

Buddleja davidii 'Summer Beauty'

One of the better butterfly bushes to come out of Holland, this cultivar was bred at Horticulture Research International in Boskoop. *Buddleja davidii* 'Summer Beauty' is a sibling of *B*. 'Pink Delight'. The flower has more red in it than 'Pink Delight', making it a deep rich pink colour, and the foliage is silvery grey. The habit is more compact than 'Pink Delight', and it only grows to a height of 1.25 m (4 ft). *Buddleja davidii* 'Summer Beauty' is reasonably well stocked by nurseries and should not be difficult to track down. USDA zones 6–9

Buddleja davidii 'Summer Rose'

This hybrid originated at Bernheim Arboretum in the United States. When Mike Dirr performed trials on *Buddleja davidii* 'Summer Rose', everyone who saw it wanted to know what it was and where they could get one. The overall growth of the plant is compact. Beautiful deep rose flowers are set against silvery leaves. Mike believes it is less hardy than other rose-coloured cultivars. *Buddleja davidii* 'Summer Rose' is not yet available in the European market, although it can be found in the United States. USDA zones 5–9

Buddleja davidii 'Three in One'

This plant is a novelty, with three distinctly coloured flowers borne on the same plant. *Buddleja davidii* 'Three in One' flowers freely from midsummer to midautumn with a mixture of white, light purple, and dark purple flowers. In my opinion the different colours make the shrub look messy and unattractive; however, other people will love it. The overall shape is compact, and there is a silvery grey cast to the young foliage, fading with age. The leaves are grey-green above and silver grey beneath. *Buddleja davidii* 'Three in One' is available in the United States. USDA zones 6–9

Buddleja davidii 'Twilight'

Mountain Valley Growers of Squaw Valley, California, raised and introduced this new cultivar. *Buddleja davidii* 'Twilight' is interesting as it extends the range of colours. The purple-pink flowers are darker than most *Buddleja davidii* cultivars. The darkness of the flower colour was inherited from its parent *B. davidii* 'Black Knight', from whom it also inherited vigour, growing to a height of 1.75–2.5 m (5.8–8.3 ft). *Buddleja davidii* 'Twilight' is not yet available in the European market, but it can be purchased from Mountain Valley Growers. USDA zones 6–9

Buddleja davidii 'Violet Message'

Originating from Holland, this cultivar is one of the smallest available, attaining a height and spread of only 1.25 m (4 ft). The compact slender plant has arching spreading branches. Young growth is silvery grey; with age the foliage turns medium green with silver undersides. The fragrant bright purple flowers are borne on panicles, reaching 30 cm (12 in), from midsummer to first frosts. *Buddleja davidii* 'Violet Message' has a bright future in the small-garden market. This cultivar may be purchased in the United States. It is not yet available in the European nursery trade, but I am sure that it will not be long before it is. USDA zones 6–9

Buddleja davidii 'White Ball'

In my opinion, this is the best dwarf *Buddleja* cultivar of them all, and it is well worth looking for if garden space is at a premium. Buddleja davidii 'White Ball' is neat, compact, and long flowering. In hot summers the plant will reach a height of 0.75–2 m (3–5 ft) with a spread of 1.5–2.25 m (5–7 ft). In the average U.K. summer, however, it seldom grows more than 1.5 m (5 ft) high and spreads 1.5 m (5 ft). Flowers are white and borne from mid to late summer or early autumn. The silver-grey foliage can have a great visual impact when planted in small odd-numbered groups against coloured foliage plants. If space is limited, then plant single specimens and use companion under plantings. *Buddleja davidii* 'White Ball' responds well to spring pruning and feeding. It is widely available in the nursery trade. USDA zones 6–9

Buddleja davidii 'White Bouquet'

The scented flowers are large and white, with yellow throat rings. The flowers soon fade to brown, however, which detracts from their beauty. *Buddleja davidii* 'White Bouquet' is a dense, low-spreading shrub that reaches less than 1.5 m (4 ft) tall. Introduced into cultivation from 1942, this is one of the better whites, and it is widely available in the trade. USDA zones 6–9

Buddleja davidii 'White Cloud'

This plant forms a medium-sized shrub. *Buddleja davidii* 'White Cloud' produces pure white flowers with yellow eyes in large broad panicles measuring 25 cm (10 in) long. The down side is that as the blooms fade, they turn brown and look unsightly. Deadheading is well worth the effort. This cultivar is available in both the United Kingdom and the United States. USDA zones 6–9

Buddleja davidii 'White Harlequin'

This cultivar arose as a chance sport of a white-flowered buddleja and is of unknown garden origin. The leaves have a creamy yellowish white margin, so *Buddleja davidii* 'White Harlequin' looks good even when not in flower. Like *Buddleja davidii* 'Harlequin', this variegated form is notorious for throwing green shoots which should be dealt with right away. If the growth is young and soft, the best way to remove it is by rubbing it off the main stem. If cut with a pair of secateurs, small dormant buds in the shoot axils will develop and more shoots will appear. A few nurseries are growing this cultivar, and it shouldn't be too difficult to source. USDA zones 7–9

Buddleja davidii 'White Profusion'

The large flower spikes measure up to 20 cm (8 in) long and bear white flowers with yellow eyes. The flowers soon fade to brown, however, and they also suffer from sun scorch during long hot summers. Overall the shrub is of a dense bushy habit, and the grey-green leaves set off the white flowers to their best advantage. When the plant is pruned in the spring, the flower spikes become extra large and long. *Buddleja davidii* 'White Profusion' was introduced into cultivation in 1945, and the Royal Horticultural Society gave it an Award of Garden Merit in 1993. Plenty of nurseries supply this cultivar, and it is well worth seeking out. USDA zones 5–9

Buddleja davidii 'White Spread'

Another Dutch hybrid, *Buddleja davidii* 'White Spread' has attractive grey-green foliage which sets off the good-sized white flower spikes. As the name suggests, the plant has a wider spread (1.2 m, 4 ft) than height (0.9 m, 3 ft). This cultivar is useful set in the middle of a mixed low-maintenance border. At present it is not listed in the *RHS Plant Finder*, although it is obtainable in Holland and Germany. It is, however, available through Longwood Gardens in the United States, and this is where the plant in the Longstock collection originated. USDA zones 5–9

Buddleja davidii 'White Wings'

Like *Buddleja davidii*, 'White Wings' has strong growth and grey-green foliage. The long panicles of white flowers are borne during mid to late summer. Only a few nurseries list *Buddleja davidii* 'White Wings', and availability might prove to be a problem. USDA zones 5–9

Buddleja davidii 'Widecombe'

I came across this plant when I visited Sir John Quicke's garden. He had bought it from Trevor Wood at Southcombe Nursery, Kewton, Exeter, Devon. The almost-glossy leaves are narrow, dark green above, and grey-green below. The deep violet-blue flowers are produced in terminal spikes. Trevor Wood raised it as a chance seedling from Widecombe Garden in the late 1970s, and he says that it is "probably best forgotten." I disagree with him, however, and I believe that it needs someone to trial it along with other forms. Sherwood Cottage Nursery, Newton St Cyres, Exeter, the new nursery run by Quicke's head gardener, is planning to stock this plant. USDA zones 5–9

Buddleja davidii 'Windy Hill'

Dennis Mareb of Windy Hill Nursery, Great Barrington, Massachusetts, raised and introduced this cultivar, which appeared in the nursery as a chance seedling. The plant has proved to be very root hardy, withstanding temperatures as low as −32°C (−25°F); although cut to the ground every year, it regrows as much as 2.5 m (8 ft) the following season. The purple flower panicles are held above slender blue-green leaves . *Buddleja davidii* 'Windy Hill' is not yet available in the European market, but it can be purchased in the United States. USDA zones 4–9

Buddleja forrestii × *B. macrostachya*

This is a naturally occurring hybrid from the Mengzi Xian region in Yunnan Province, China; it was described by Leeuwenberg (1979, p. 149). The hybrid has several characteristics from both parents. The young shoots are quadrangular in cross section with a narrow wing at each angle running the length between the nodes. The leaves are elliptic to narrowly elliptic, measuring 10–20 cm (4–8 in) long by 3–7 cm (1.25–2.75 in) wide; they are covered with fine grey woolly hair which persists until maturity. The petiole is 1.5 cm (0.6 in) long. Flowers are purple to pink and are usually in panicles. *Buddleja forrestii* × *B. macrostachya* is not common in cultivation. USDA zones 9–10

Buddleja globosa 'Cally Orange'

Michael Wickenden collected wild *Buddleja* seed in 1987 during a trip to the Lake District of central Chile. Upon his return the seeds were sown, grown on, and assessed during flowering. *Buddleja globosa* 'Cally Orange' had, in his eyes, the best flower colour and form, and he named it after his beloved Cally Gardens in Scotland. This selection has large flower-heads of deep orange blooms, sweetly scented rather like honey. USDA zones 5–9

Buddleja globosa 'Lemon Ball'

This cultivar is a relatively fast-growing shrub of rounded habit, reaching a height of 3–6 m (10–20 ft). The foliage is dark green. The lemon yellow flowers are paler than *Buddleja globosa* and are produced a little later than the species, namely in spring. *Buddleja globosa* 'Lemon Ball' is not common in cultivation. USDA zones 8–9

Buddleja ×griffithii

This naturally occurring hybrid is thought to be a cross between *Buddleja candida* and *B. macrostachya*. It was collected in Qinghai and Xizang Provinces, eastern Bangladesh, and Bhutan at elevations of 700–800 m (2300–2600 ft) and was named and described by C. B. Clarke in 1930. *Buddleja ×griffithii* is a shrub or small tree growing to a height of 6 m (20 ft). The leaves are 4–27 cm (1.5–10.5 in) long by 1–12 cm (0.5–4.5 in) wide, and both leaf surfaces are covered with fine grey hairs. The blue flowers have orange throats and are arranged in terminal and axillary panicles. *Buddleja ×griffithii* is not in common cultivation. USDA zones 9–10

Buddleja indica × B. madagascariensis

According to A. J. M. Leeuwenberg (1979), this hybrid was collected in the wild during an expedition to the Grand Basin in Réunion, a small group of islands north of Madagascar. The plant has leaves similar to *Buddleja indica* but they are narrower and longer. The flowers are similar to *B. indica* but have more flowers in the spike. The reference by Leeuwenberg is the only written record of the cross. This hybrid is not in general cultivation. USDA zones 8–10

Buddleja ×intermedia

This natural hybrid was found in France in a batch of seedlings; it is thought to be a cross between *Buddleja japonica* and *B. lindleyana*. The plant spreads by underground suckers. The light green leaves are 15 cm (6 in) long; the violet flowers are borne in drooping panicles up to 25 cm (10 in) long. *Buddleja ×intermedia* is not in cultivation in Britain, although it can be purchased in the United States. USDA zones 8–9

Buddleja ×intermedia 'Insignis'

A selection from a batch of seedlings, *Buddleja ×intermedia* 'Insignis' is thought to be a chance cross between *Buddleja japonica* and *B. lindleyana*. The leaves are 15 cm (6 in) long; the flowers are rose-violet and produced in dense erect spikes up to 15 cm (6 in) long. *Buddleja ×intermedia* 'Insignis' is not in cultivation in Britain. USDA zones 8–9

Buddleja ×lewisiana

Introduced into cultivation in 1958, this hybrid is a cross between *B. madagascariensis* ♀ and *Buddleja asiatica* ♂. It was described and named by T. H. Everett in 1947. I strongly believe, however, that it should be classified as *Buddleja madagasiatica* var. *lewisiana* because it has the same parentage. *Buddleja ×lewisiana* is a loose, spreading, and lax shrub up to 2 m (6.5 ft) in height. The young shoots are densely felted with white hairs; the leaves are lanceolate, up to 17 cm (6.75 in) long, and densely felted with white hairs. The flowers are white in bud, opening yellow or orange in panicles up to 20 cm (8 in) long on terminal shoots. The dry seed capsule persists for a long time. In the Longstock collection *Buddleja ×lewisiana* has proved to be tender, requiring winter protection. I grow it in a 25-L (15-in) pot and bring it in for the winter in mid to late autumn. USDA zones 8–9

Buddleja lindleyana hybrids

Some of the problems with *Buddleja lindleyana* is that it grows large and untidy, and tends to sucker everywhere if conditions are favourable. These traits must be considered when choosing this plant, as it colonizes large areas of a garden in one or two seasons. What could it do if it escaped? *Buddleja lindleyana* and all its hybrids are only root hardy in the United Kingdom, apart from some of the more favourable areas such as the west coast, with balmy weather influenced by the Gulf Stream. The *B. lindleyana* hybrid plants in the Longstock collection came from the Bernheim Arboretum for trials, and are not yet available in the European market.

Buddleja lindleyana 'Avent', *B. lindleyana* 'Gloster', *B. lindleyana* 'Mayflower', and *B. lindleyana* 'Miss Vicie' are four new cultivars raised in the United States. They were selected for their smaller stature and more compact flower spikes. In U.S. trials these plants reached 1.75 m (5.8 ft) in one season and are described as aggressive colonizers. Deep cobalt blue flowers are displayed on long, narrow, pendant, arching panicles, similar to a miniature wisteria. The tubular flowers are interesting close up but are disappointing as an overall floral display. The spent flower-heads fade with dignity—a good trait for breeders to import into the showy and flamboyant *Buddleja davidii* hybrids. These hybrids are not yet available in the European market, although they may be purchased in the United States. USDA zones 7–9

Buddleja 'Lochinch'

This hybrid came from the garden of the Earl of Stair at Lochinch in Wigtownshire, Scotland, and it is a cross between *Buddleja davidii* and *B. fallowiana*. *Buddleja* 'Lochinch' is one of my favourite *Buddleja* hybrids. The grey-green foliage is the perfect setting for showing off the blue flowers; the result is an outstanding and beautiful colour combination. The best features of both parents are brought to the fore. With *B. fallowiana* in its parentage, this hybrid has silvery broad leaves, and the *B. davidii* gives it the added hardiness along with the best flower shape and colour. Its flowering period is slightly later than other *B. davidii* hybrids, starting in midsummer, and in mild areas it may retain its leaves through winter. The graceful arching branches have narrow panicles of sweetly scented, light lavender heliotrope blue flowers. The Royal Horticultural Society gave *Buddleja* 'Lochinch' an Award of Garden Merit in 1993. This very popular hybrid is common in cultivation and should be easy to find in any good shrub nursery. USDA zones 6–8

Buddleja madagasiatica 'Margaret Pike'

Syn. *Buddleja ×lewisiana* 'Margaret Pike'

A cross between *Buddleja madagascariensis* ♀ and *B. asiatica* ♂ gave rise to the hybrid *B. madagasiatica* 'Margaret Pike'. The cross was made by A. V. Pike at Hever Castle in 1951, and Pike's description of the plant, along with photographs, was published in *Gardeners' Chronicle* on 19 April 1953. The plant grows to a height of 2 m (6.5 in) with a loose spreading habit. The flower trusses of *B. madagasiatica* 'Margaret Pike' are up to 22 cm (8.75 in) long and 18 cm (7.25 in) wide. The flowers open a clear primrose yellow, turning buff a few days later. The scent is like that of *B. asiatica*. This hybrid is slightly hardier than both parents and has proved to be root hardy. USDA zones 7–9

Buddleja ×pikei

This hybrid resulted from a cross between *Buddleja alternifolia* ♀ × *B. caryopteridifolia* ♂, possibly backcrossed with *B. crispa*. It was named and described in 1950 by Harold Fletcher, who was the Regius Keeper at the Royal Botanic Garden, Edinburgh. *Buddleja ×pikei* is a free-flowering, straggling, deciduous shrub up to a height of 1.5 m (4 ft). Its leaves are opposite, up to 15 cm (6 in) long, and usually narrowly lanceolate scalloped to lobed. The flowers are mauve-pink with orange throats borne in long terminal, often leafy, panicles. This is a very useful free-flowering shrub for a sunny, warm position. Prune in spring when required. The plant in the Longstock collection flowered regularly and usually aroused some interest among the visitors. *Buddleja ×pikei* is not common in cultivation, but it is worth seeking. USDA zones 7–9

Buddleja ×pikei 'Hever'

This cultivar is the result of a cross between *Buddleja alternifolia* ♀ and *B. caryopteridifolia* ♂ created by A. V. Pike of Hever Castle Gardens in Kent. *Buddleja ×pikei* 'Hever' is the most popular selection from this cross. The foliage is like *B. caryopteridifolia* in the lower part of the shrub, with age becoming more like *B. alternifolia* higher up. The distinction between the two forms of foliage become more pronounced when plants are pruned heavily to encourage strong vigorous growth: the first six or seven leaves are similar to *B. caryopteridifolia*, while those beyond are the shape of *B. alternifolia*. The plant is deciduous and has an upright habit to 2 m (6.5 ft). *Buddleja ×pikei* 'Hever' is totally hardy to −15°C (5°F) and flowers on the current year's growth. This buddleja is very good as a cut flower and will last for up to ten days in a display. Although not common in cultivation, plants are stocked by a few specialist nurseries. USDA zones 7–9

Buddleja 'Pink Delight'

One of the best *Buddleja* hybrids to come out of Holland, this was bred at Horticulture Research International in Boskoop. To me 'Pink Delight' is one of the best and prettiest of all the pink-flowered hybrids. I first saw it in a garden in the Loire region back in 1990, and I was attracted to the compact shrub with beautiful fragrant pink plumes up to 30 cm (12 in) long set against silvery grey foliage. The ultimate height is 1.75 m (5.8 ft), with a spread of 2 m (6.5 ft). This was given the Royal Horticultural Society's Award of Garden Merit in 1993. USDA zones 6–9

Buddleja 'Salmon Spheres'

Steve Nevard, a keen hobby plant breeder, used *Buddleja globosa* as one of the parents in breeding this hybrid. The round salmon pink flowers are produced in terminal clusters, the same as *B. globosa* but much, much smaller in size. The flowers are without scent and do not have a repeat flush. The general growth of the shrub is not as vigorous as *B. globosa*. It is not common in cultivation. USDA zones 6–9

Buddleja 'Silver Frost'

This is a new hybrid from the Mike Dirr stable in Athens, Georgia, U.S.A. *Buddleja* 'Silver Frost' has outstanding silver-grey foliage with white upright flower panicles. This hybrid is unusual because one of its parents is *Buddleja* 'Lochinch', which has blue flowers, but the blue traits seem to be recessive in 'Silver Frost'. The plant grows to a height of 2 m (6.5 ft). I have not seen 'Silver Frost' in the flesh, but I will be in the queue to get the first one as I think that it looks like a winner. It is not yet available in the European market, although it can be purchased in the United States. USDA zones 5–9

Buddleja ×wardii

This is a naturally occurring hybrid between *Buddleja alternifolia* and *B. crispa*; it was named and described by C. Marquand in 1929. This plant was collected in south-eastern Xizang, China, where it grows into a shrub or small tree 1–5 m (3–16 ft). Leaves are sometimes alternate and sometimes opposite on the same plant, even on the same stem. The leaf characteristics are a mixture of both parents' and the leaves are covered with grey hairs. The flowers are a light mauve to purple-lilac with orange throats. *Buddleja* ×*wardii* is not common in cultivation and could be difficult to find. USDA zones 8–9

Buddleja 'West Hill'

This is a hybrid between *Buddleja davidii* and *B. fallowiana*. This cross was done some years ago at the Earl of Stair's Lochinch Garden in Wigtownshire, Scotland. Two plants were released into the commercial sector: *Buddleja* 'Lochinch' and *Buddleja* 'West Hill'. The flowers of *Buddleja* 'West Hill' are violet to lilac with orange eyes; they are produced in terminal panicles from late spring to midautumn. The foliage is similar to both parents, and the shoots and leaves are densely covered in whitish grey hairs. USDA zones 5–9

Buddleja ×*weyeriana*

In 1914 Mr. Van de Weyer at Smedmore House, Corfe Castle, Dorset made this cross between *Buddleja davidii* var. *magnifica* and *B. globosa*. The resulting seedlings proved to be a mixed bag of plants, giving rise to many hybrids. *Buddleja* ×*weyeriana* 'Golden Glow' and *B.* ×*weyeriana* 'Moonlight' are but two. Their strongest genetic features came from *B. globosa*. *Buddleja* ×*weyeriana* is a deciduous shrub similar to *B. globosa* in growth habit but generally not as tall. The flowers are much later than *B. globosa*, being borne in late summer to early autumn. They are light yellow, tinged with pink to violet, and produced in spherical heads in tight terminal clusters on the current year's growth. This hybrid should be pruned in the spring. USDA zones 7–9

Buddleja ×*weyeriana* 'Elstead Hybrid'

Resulting from a cross made in 1921 between *Buddleja davidii* var. *magnifica* and *Buddleja globosa*, 'Elstead Hybrid' is a deciduous shrub similar to *B. globosa*, although the flowers appear much later. They are light yellow, tinged pink to violet, with a brown throat. Spherical heads are arranged in tight terminal clusters on the current year's growth. In my experience, this cultivar is inferior to many other *Buddleja* ×*weyeriana*. It is not common in cultivation and not listed in the *RHS Plant Finder*, although several U.S. outlets offer it for sale. USDA zones 7–9

Buddleja ×weyeriana 'Golden Glow'

This was a result of a cross made in 1914 by Mr. Van de Weyer at Smedmore House, Corfe Castle, Dorset between *Buddleja davidii* var. *magnifica* and *B. globosa*. The resulting seedlings proved to be a mixed bag of plants, and the strongest genetic features came from *B. globosa*. The plant has a lax and open habit. When pruned regularly, *Buddleja ×weyeriana* 'Golden Glow' reaches 1.2–1.5 m (4–5 ft). The foliage is dark olive green above with a silvery tone underneath. Its golden orange flowers are borne from midsummer to early autumn. This cultivar should be pruned in the spring. Many nurseries list and stock *Buddleja ×weyeriana* 'Golden Glow'. USDA zones 7–9

Buddleja ×weyeriana 'Honeycomb'

A deciduous shrub with a rounded spreading habit, blue-green leaves, and sweetly scented flowers, which in bud are creamy yellow—without a lavender tinge—opening to a beautiful golden yellow with a deep butterscotch centre. *Buddleja ×weyeriana* 'Honeycomb' outperforms its *B. ×weyeriana* stable mates in several ways: it is a stronger grower, it has better leaf colour, its flowers are fragrant, and it is easier to grow.

This hybrid originated in Aberdeenshire, Scotland, from an unknown breeder, although it certainly has *Buddleja globosa* and *B. davidii* in its parentage. In 1995 Mike Dirr bought a plant from Crathes Castle, a National Trust property in Scotland, as an unnamed *Buddleja davidii*. Upon his return to Georgia, it flowered in the test plots. To Dirr's surprise, it was a very good form with yellow flowers, and the plant was voted the best buddleja in the plots. Material was distributed to nurserymen, and Mark Griffith at Griffith Propagation Nursery came up with the name 'Honeycomb'. Terriflorida has grown it for one year in Florida (zone 9); despite temperatures of −2°C (28°F), the plants have never been without flowers all year. *Buddleja ×weyeriana* 'Honeycomb' is sometimes damaged by frost, however, it is root hardy in colder areas. Prune this cultivar in the spring to encourage larger flowers and to shape.

Here we have a Scottish plant bought and named by Americans, now about to be launched into the European market. All I know is that *Buddleja*

×*weyeriana* 'Honeycomb' is a great plant, and someone in Scotland did not appreciate its true value. I saw a specimen on trial at the Sir Harold Hillier Gardens and Arboretum planted in the most prominent place—the main entrance to the visitors' centre. USDA zones 8–10

Buddleja ×weyeriana 'Lady de Ramsey'

This is a deciduous shrub similar to *Buddleja globosa* in growth habit but generally not as tall. The light yellow flowers are tinged pink to violet and are borne much later than *B. globosa*, in late summer and early autumn. They are produced in spherical heads arranged in tight terminal clusters on the current year's growth. Plants should be pruned in the spring. *Buddleja* ×*weyeriana* 'Lady de Ramsey' is not easy to tell apart from *Buddleja* ×*weyeriana*. This old hybrid is not common in cultivation, and it may prove difficult to find. USDA zones 6–9

Buddleja ×weyeriana 'Moonlight'

This is another of the *Buddleja davidii* var. *magnifica* × *B. globosa* crosses made by Mr. Van de Weyer at Smedmore House in 1914. The colours in the flower of *Buddleja* ×*weyeriana* 'Moonlight' reflect the name well: they are soft pale yellow tinged, dark dusky pink to soft violet-red. The flowers are much later than *B. globosa*, being produced in late summer to early autumn. They are borne in spherical heads arranged in tight terminal clusters on the current year's growth. Prune in the spring if required. *Buddleja* ×*weyeriana* 'Moonlight' is not common in cultivation. USDA zone 6

Buddleja ×weyeriana 'Sungold'

Raised in Holland in 1966, this is the result of another cross between *Buddleja davidii* var. *magnifica* and *B. globosa*. *Buddleja* ×*weyeriana* 'Sungold' is superior to *Buddleja* ×*weyeriana* 'Golden Glow', as the flowers are a richer and clearer colour. The golden yellow flowers flushed with orange are held in spherical heads, which are rather acute at the apex, in tight terminal clusters. Prune in the spring. *Buddleja* ×*weyeriana* 'Sungold' was given the Royal Horticultural Society's Award of Garden Merit in 1993. It is widely available throughout the European nursery market and may be purchased in the United States as well. USDA zones 7–9

Buddleja ×*weyeriana* 'Wattle Bird'

This stunningly different buddleja was bred in Australia. It produces spikes of golden yellow flowers from midsummer to midautumn, which are very long by ×*weyeriana* standards. The shrub grows to a height of 3.6 m (12 ft) and a spread of 2.7 m (9 ft) and has greyish green foliage. USDA zones 5–9

Buddleja ×*whiteana*

R. J. Moore performed this cross between *Buddleja asiatica* ♀ and *B. alternifolia* ♂. This hybrid was named in honour of Dr. Orlando E. White, director of botany at the experimental farm of the University of Virginia. The shrub has a lax open habit and grows to a height of 1.8–2.4 m (6–8 ft) with a spread of 1.2–1.8 m (4–6 ft). The leaf colour ranges from greyish to silvery green. The flowers are pale lilac, almost white, with bright orange throats. This plant is not in common cultivation. USDA zone 8

Buddleja 'Wind Tor'

Overall, this plant is similar to *Buddleja* 'Lochinch' but has much darker flowers. They are deep violet-blue with orange eyes, making a striking contrast. *Buddleja* 'Wind Tor' was raised in a private garden at Widecombe in Devon, and I sourced a plant from Greenway Garden when it was still in private ownership. *Buddleja* 'Wind Tor' is uncommon in cultivation and not easy to source; however, I understand that it is available in Holland. I feel that this plant is a good hybrid and should be kept going. USDA zones 5–9

Buddleja 'Winter Sun'

This hybrid resulted from a cross between *Buddleja nappii* and *B. officinalis*. It was raised by Steve Nevard, who gave it to me for the Longstock collection in the mid-1990s. The flowers have a shape similar to those of *B.* ×*weyeriana* hybrids. They are salmon pink, flushed with a soft primrose yellow, with orange throats, giving them a dusky look. The main flush of colour is during the early part of the year, when the daylight period lengthens. Like its parent *B. officinalis*, the flowers are beautifully scented. The leaves of *Buddleja* 'Winter Sun' are rough on both surfaces, and the young shoots are covered in fine coppery grey hairs. Because the plant has *B. officinalis* parentage, I decided to grow this one in a large pot among the other half-hardy buddlejas, which stand outside for the summer and are brought in for the winter around mid to late autumn. It would be a good plant for the conservatory. Hardiness is untested but I would think it to be about similar to *B. nappii.* This plant is not in common cultivation. USDA zones 7–9

Chapter 3
Care and Cultivation

During a trip to China in 2001, I visited Sleepy Dragon Nature Reserve, the only area in the world where giant pandas still live in the wild. The nature reserve is 200,000 ha (500,000 acres) of forest set in the mountains of Sichuan Province. It was beside the Min He near the research station that, to my great delight, I saw my first wild Asian buddleja. I took a good look around the woodland in the area and I was amazed and distracted by all of the wonderful plants that we grow as cherished garden gems in Britain. Here I was, surrounded by them, growing as weeds in their natural habitat. As I walked away from the river into the forest, however, the trail of the buddleja soon got cold, and I had to retrace my steps to find them again. In the wild buddlejas seem to require lots of sunlight, moisture, and very little competition from other woody shrubby plants.

In their natural habitats, buddlejas are pioneers and can get a roothold in the most unexpected places. Buddlejas have very simple requirements to grow, and it is this frugality that has made *Buddleja davidii* such a loveable rogue, sprouting from crumbling brickwork, railway embankments, road verges, and demolition sites. In the wild buddlejas are usually found along watercourses among the stones and shingles and sometimes from thin cracks in stones.

Success in growing buddlejas depends on a very few crucial but essential ingredients. First and most importantly, the soil must be free draining. Buddleja do not thrive in cold wet soil, and plants will quickly die under such conditions. Over the years I have gone to inspect people's dead or dying plants only to find that they have spent the winter in water-logged soil. This is the most common cause of death for pot-grown and open-grown buddlejas. The majority of *Buddleja* species come from relatively warm climates. I ask you to put yourself in the life of a buddleja: although it would be all right during the summer months, how would you like to spend the winter in an unheated swimming pool in Britain? Strong wind also can be detrimental to their health. Not only will it break branches, strong wind will cause the plant to sway to and fro, which creates an elongated hole in the soil around the neck of the plant. This may cause root damage, including damage to the main support roots. During the winter when the ground is frozen, water collects and freezes in the elongated hole in the soil, crushing the main stem.

Soil Requirements

Apart from ascertaining that the soil is free draining, the other important factor that any keen gardener should find out is the pH of the soil. The pH reflects the acidity or alkalinity of a solution and is measured on a scale from 0 to 14. Neutral solutions, such as deionized water, have a pH of 7. Going towards the alkaline end of the range, household soap has a pH of 9–9.5, milk of magnesium has a pH of 11, and caustic soda has a pH of 13. Going the other way, human skin has a pH of 5.5, lemon juice has a pH of 3.5, and car battery acid has a pH of 2. Most garden soils fall between pH values of 5.5 to 8.5. Thankfully, buddlejas are happy throughout this range, and perform equally well in acid or alkaline soils.

Although buddlejas are pioneering plants and survive in poor soils, they perform best when nutrients are freely available. This is where knowing the pH becomes important as the pH of the soil affects the availability of nutrients held in various chemical forms. In acid or low-pH soils, lime (calcium and magnesium) is lacking and other important nutrients become unavailable to the buddleja. The result is a very slow-growing, compact plant. To help improve the pH conditions, add ground limestone to the soil at 600 g per m² (1.5 lb per square yard) for heavy clay soil, 400 g per m² (1.0 lb per square yard) for loamy soil, and 200 g per m² (0.5 lb per square yard) for light sandy soil. These amounts will raise the pH by 1. Be careful not to overdose the soil with limestone in any given year.

In very alkaline soil, calcium, magnesium, and most of the main nutrients are freely available, however iron, manganese, zinc, copper, boron, and several other trace elements are locked up. Iron is a vital ingredient for plant life and when it becomes unavailable, lime-hating plants—calcifuges—such as rhododendrons struggle to gain enough iron and may develop alkaline-induced chlorosis, a lack of chlorophyll. This condition shows itself as yellowing of the leaves, interveinal at first but quickly spreading to the whole leaf. In contrast lime-tolerant plants—calcicoles—are better able to cope with high levels of calcium, and are more adept at extracting iron and other essential elements from alkaline soil. To decrease the pH by 1 in alkaline soils, flowers of sulphur should be worked in at the following rate: 150 g per m^2 (6 oz per square yard) for heavy clay soils, 100 g per m^2 (4 oz per square yard) for loamy soils, and 75 g per m^2 (3 oz per square yard) for light sandy soils. This should be done at least three to four months prior to planting, so the sulphur has time to lock up the freely available calcium, thereby reducing its effect. Chelated iron and acid fertilizers, such as sulphate of ammonia, will also help lower the pH.

Compared with acid soils alkaline soils have a much more active flora and fauna, such as fungal mycorrhizae and earthworms. It is thanks to these life forms that organic matter quickly disappears from one year to the next. I personally think that the white or silver hairs on buddleja leaves and stems are better on plants grown in alkaline soils, often shown to best advantage on *Buddleja nivea*. The scientific explanation is that the free calcium in the soil aids the plant in the production of these hairs. The hairs have two functions: to deter browsing animals from eating them and to reduce water loss through the leaf pores, or stomata.

Another soil factor to consider is drainage. Buddlejas must have a free-draining soil, otherwise the roots quickly die back and rot, often beyond recovery. In Hampshire the soil is often a thin layer of organic loam over deep chalk, and it is an extremely hungry soil which quickly devours whatever organic matter is applied. With time and the addition of tonnes of organic matter, such soils become rich in beneficial microorganisms conducive to healthy plants. When a garden requires vast quantities of organic material to improve its fertility, look for whatever is inexpensive and locally available in large quantities.

I strongly believe in encouraging nature's gardeners, the "hidden army," beneath our feet. The main soil improver is the humble earthworm, which chews through tonnes of soil, mixing inorganic with organic matter, and passing the mix through its gut to come out much improved, all of which aids sustainable plant growth. Fungi, bacteria, and other members of the subterranean world work wonders in improving the overall fertility of soils. Laying mulches and incorporating organic material such as farmyard manure will encourage a rich and diverse flora and fauna in the soil.

Organic Material and Fertilizers

Buddlejas are easy-going plants but they perform best when they are well fed, and to this end most soils will benefit from the addition of copious amounts of organic material—usually the more the better. Volume for volume, the price of organic materials is about one-tenth that of potting composts. Be careful when using any organic or animal waste, as it usually comes unrotted and with a pungent smell, and you will become the talk of the neighbourhood. It is advisable to stack farmyard manure in a mound, cover it with sheeting, and let it compost for at least a year prior to use. This composting will avoid scorching young roots and shoots due to the reduction of nitrogen during the composting process. (It is always advisable to compost farmyard manure for one to three years before using it in the garden.) Another reason for composting the manure is that more nutrients and trace elements are available to the plants. However, with all these organic manures the nutrient content will be variable.

Farmyard manure

Well-composted farmyard manure is almost black, and the straw and odours should be hardly identifiable. When farmyard manure is fresh it is referred to as being "long" and when composted it is "short." To me there is nothing better that good-quality composted cow farmyard manure. The quality is superior to that of any other nutrient source, and it helps condition the soil by adding plenty of organic matter along with vital nutrients and trace elements. The most common farmyard manure is cow manure. Very often it is from the calf pens emptied in the spring, when the calves are let out to the fields. The manure and straw are usually well mixed by the calves. Dairy cow manure is scraped and washed into a slurry pit and is sprayed onto the farmers' fields throughout the year. I know first hand, living close to a dairy, and I am at the wrong end of the south-westerly winds in the smell department. Chicken, turkey, and pig manure is also available, with horse manure less so these days.

Farmyard manure stacked for composting should be covered with plastic sheeting and should have some way of keeping the excess liquid ("lade" as my journeyman told me more than thirty years ago) from running off into waterways. In addition to avoiding polluted waterways, containing the runoff will help with the break down of the manure. Used in a diluted form as a regular general liquid feed, a solution of composted manure gives the best fruit and vegetables; in my opinion the best-tasting tomatoes always come from vines fed with lade. The only thing I do not like about farmyard manure is the amount of weed seeds it carries. I do feel, however, that what it adds to the soil is well worth the effort of picking a few unwanted seedlings.

Local riding stables are often a good source of horse manure. I always prefer this to be composted for at least twelve to twenty-four months prior to use to help break it down into suitable ingredients. Some stables use wood shavings for horsebox litter. In the long term, the shavings produce a more even consistency when composted. One drawback with straw-bedded horses is that there tends to be a large quantity of straw relative to manure and it can take longer to compost down.

The waste of chicken, pheasant, duck, goose, and turkey manure—or hen pen—is being snapped up by mushroom growers for their culture compost. Chickens and other fowl extract very little nutrients from their food, with the excess passed into their manure. In addition, the digestive system of birds relies on strong, high-nitrate acids to break down their food. This is why hen pen is so nitrogen-rich. When fresh, bird manure is too high in nitrogen and will cause soft, weak plant growth. Chicken manure is commercially available in pelletted form.

Guano

Over the centuries seabird colonies have left large deposits of guano, a posh name for droppings, which is basically the same as hen pen, although stronger and with a fishy smell. Other sources of guano are also commercially available, from bats for example. When using guano, do remember its nitrogen content is very high. A little goes a long way, and it should be used in small amounts. It is better to put a second or third application than burning and killing plants with too large an initial application.

Seaweed

Many maritime gardens make full use of this natural product, as tonnes and tonnes are washed ashore annually. Seaweed is a very popular fertilizer and compost material with coastal gardeners on the western coast of Britain, namely Scotland and Ireland. Once composted it provides the soil with super fertility. The most positive characteristic of seaweed is that it is very difficult to overdose to the stage of plant scorch. Seaweed is a rich source of nitrogen and vital trace elements such as iron and iodine. Seaweed meal can be purchased; however, it gets everywhere. Several commercially available fertilizers are based on seaweed. These organic products, correctly diluted, are quickly taken up by the plant and are supposed to improve microbial activity. I used seaweed meal successfully at Pollok Country Park, when I was renovating and regenerating the Rhododendron Woodland Garden, by top-dressing the root pan (rooting area) of the rhododendrons to stimulate the soil microorganisms beneficial to good plant growth, and it is equally beneficial for the buddlejas that have a similarly shallow fibrous rooting habit. After spending a day spreading seaweed meal, however, there was never any bother getting a seat on the bus home as the smell clings to you and your clothing for some time.

Fish meal

Fish has been used as a fertilizer for centuries around the world. When fishermen return with the catch, the unusable parts of the fish such as bones, skin, heads as well as undesirable species are put to one side for safe disposal by the fertilizer companies. Fish meal is a rich source of nitrogen and other vital trace elements such as iron and iodine.

Blood and bone

These natural by-products of the slaughterhouse have lost their popularity due to mad cow disease and anthrax. When I signed up for the studentship at the Royal Botanic Garden, Edinburgh, the gardens' administration asked me to prove I had my tetanus and anthrax injections and that they were recent. Laws require that bone meal sold in garden centres and nurseries must be sterilized to reduce these health risks.

Dried blood is rich in iron and essential trace elements, and bone meal is rich in calcium and other essential trace elements. Both are naturally quite smelly, and after applying them the smell can linger in the area for some time—and the same applies to the person applying it. Some people advise not to use bone meal on alkaline soils as it compounds the problems associated with alkaline nutrient lockup.

Mushroom compost

Mushroom farms always have a problem with disposal of spent compost, and they often sell it at a modest rate (usually enough to cover their transport and labour costs). Our local mushroom farm uses hen pen mixed with locally grown straw to produce the base compost, whereas some other mushroom composts are based on horse manure. The cultivated mushroom is a commercial hybrid and does not exist in the wild, so responsible mushroom farms steam and sterilize the outgoing compost. When fresh it is light and fluffy, and pieces of straw and white mycelium (threadlike fungal growth) can still be recognized. The compost also contains gypsum, a form of calcium, as part of the top casing. The ideal is to stack fresh compost and store it under a cover for nine to twelve months prior to use; when it turns black and the smell and straw can no longer be identified, it is ready to use. Bagged mushroom compost is also available through garden centres and nurseries.

When the compost is fresh, several nutrients are in excess of any plant's requirements. These elements can become toxic, scorching or burning plants such as herbaceous perennials. In addition, mushroom compost is not recommended for acid-loving plants. People have often asked me if there is any nutrient value to mushroom compost, and I say, "How can something that smells so bad contain nothing of value?" The compost has nitrogen, which is slowly released as it decomposes, as well as many vital trace elements for successful healthy plant growth. Mushroom compost is an inexpensive soil amendment that adds organic material.

Distillery and brewery waste products

Spent hops and mash from a brewery are another good source of organic material. This was used in the Royal Botanic Garden, Edinburgh, when I was a student there. One drawback in using it is that the neighbours might think that you have been at the beer. The smell is unpopular, and the greenfinches get in your way as they stagger about on the heap quite intoxicated. From a gardening point of view, the hops tend to clump together in a soggy sticky mess and are not easy to break up and apply as a mulch. During dry weather they dry out to form hard clods, which are difficult to break up. The birds love to have a good old rummage through the mulch once out in the garden and spread the mulch onto the paths, lawn, or patio, making it look untidy. During dry summers a discarded cigarette can set fire to the mulch, and it will smoulder and creep through the border with devastating effects. We had such a case in Edinburgh, and we were all surprised as to how much damage can be done by something as small as a cigarette end in such a short time. By the time we had assembled the hoses, over half the bed was smouldering and the resulting plant loss was disastrous.

Leaf litter

There are few gardens in the world that do not generate copious amounts of organic material, including leaf litter. Among gardeners leaf litter, or leaf-mould, is known as the Rolls Royce of composts. Although leaf litter composting takes much longer due to the fact that it is a cool process as fungi break down the leaves, as opposed to the traditional compost heap which generates heat and is broken down by bacteria.

Wood chippings

I have been a great fan of wood chippings for the past two decades, as it is the ultimate way in recycling a renewable green resource that would normally be burned. Most gardens produce copious amounts of woody debris, which can be put through a chipper and recycled in the garden. Wood chippers come in a variety of shapes, sizes, and prices. If you feel the cost of buying one is too much, group together with some friends or neighbours to share the cost. Wood chippers can also be rented, together with safety equipment including ear defenders, goggles, and thick leather gloves.

When I was working at the Longstock Park Gardens, the chippings were mounded up in one of our Heston straw-bale bays and the heap was turned once or twice a year before it was used as mulch. The heap can become very, very hot, with the centre becoming very dry. The main down side of chipping mulch is that in the summer during prolonged periods of hot dry weather the mulch can easily be set on fire. Often the source of combustion is a carelessly discarded cigarette end.

Bark chippings

The bark used for chipping originates from conifers and is removed from the trunk during the early stages of processing at the sawmill. Conifer bark is very high in resin. When fresh and dry, it can be very flammable as volatile gases are given off during very hot dry weather, and these can ignite with drastic results. Bark comes in various sizes and states of decomposition, depending on the intended use. Larger chips take longer to break down; however, the look is very rough and not ideally suited to the domestic garden finish. Fine particle sizes are ideal for soil conditioning and propagation compost.

Cocoa shells

This mulch has been available commercially for well over the last decade. As a mulch it is very pleasing to look at and when damp has the smell of chocolate. The shells are mechanically shredded into small round shapes and are proving to be resistant to breakdown, outlasting other mulches. With maturity it goes a very dark brown to black colour. Although a recycled material with nutrient value, it is transported across the world, which takes its environmental toll.

Shoddy

Shoddy is a by-product of the textile industry and is little used nowadays, although it did have its place in the history of horticulture. Shoddy is composed of the threads and small offcuts from the weaving machines. It takes a very long time to produce suitable compost from this material. Traditionally, it was incorporated into the bottom of the trench during the annual plot digging. Shoddy also can be homemade from cotton, linen, or woollen clothes which have been shredded at the end of their useful lives.

Grass cuttings

Many people like to recycle their garden waste, and I always encourage this practice. Grass clippings on their own are to be avoided, however, as they tend to form a slimy smelly mass. When composting grass clippings, always mix them with plenty of other drier vegetative material, such as shredded prunings or paper. The clippings are high in nitrogen and help to break down the drier carbon-rich materials into suitable compost. After treatment with hormone weed killers lawn clippings should not be added to the compost heap for at least a month to six weeks, as they still contain active hormone weed killer and will contaminate the compost; hormone weed killer has a very long life and can be passed to other plants in this way. All too often I have seen hormone weed killer damage perennial herbaceous and shrubby plants through treated grass clippings, even after a year of composting.

Bio-tea

The development of bio-tea is proving to be one of the best things to come out of Holland since Gouda and Edam cheese, clogs, and Dutch beer. This product was widely used by Victorian gardeners. During my apprenticeship I recall using lade, which was produced by placing a sack full of the blackest best cow dung in an old bathtub full of water. The resulting foul-smelling green liquid was diluted to the colour of medium strength tea and applied as a liquid fertilizer and foliar feed to a wide variety of glasshouse plants. This lade produced the healthiest, strongest, and tastiest plants that I have ever come across.

During the last three to four years there has been a lot of research carried out in Holland and Belgium into similar products with similar outstanding results. Bio-tea is made from completely organic substances brewed in a special vat, with temperature control and a lot of aeration to supply the microorganisms with ample oxygen to multiply. After twenty-four hours in this aerated and warm environment, the brew is ready to use. The bio-tea solution is then diluted and applied to the crop. The easiest method is to add it inline with the irrigation system line using a diluter. Bio-tea is high in beneficial microorganisms, which control diseases and promote strong well-balanced growth.

Domestic green waste compost

Horticulturists, gardeners, organic farmers, and landscape industries all use commercially produced green waste compost. A renewable environmentally friendly by-product from the waste management process is produced commercially to a variety of physical and chemical specifications. Once organic debris is sorted from the main collection, it is transported to the composting centres. Each load is visually inspected for inorganic materials such as plastic, glass, stones, and metal and is passed through a milling machine which grinds everything up into small shards. It is then mounded up into large long windrows and regularly turned with a huge bucketed machine. The key to the whole process is regularly introducing air and water into the huge mounds of green waste to secure and sustain aerobic microorganism activity. Water and liquid run off from the windrows is collected, treated, and recycled back into the process. This process lasts up to ten to twelve weeks and the mounds reach a temperature of 70°C (185°F). This is sufficient to sterilize the compost, as weeds and seeds cannot withstand the high temperatures. Maturation follows the composting phase; this is when the complex materials are broken down and toxic levels fall. The compost is allowed to settle and cool and is checked to ensure complete conversion of all organic material into compost.

This commercially produced compost is sterile, uniform, and odourless and contains 1.3 per cent nitrogen, 0.25 per cent phosphorus, and 0.75 per cent potassium, with a pH of 8. When it is freshly delivered, however, it is very dusty to handle. At Longstock we solved the problem by leaving it out in the rain to overwinter before we top-dressed the garden in the spring. Another problem with this produce is that when it is mulched out on top of a bed it compacts down with rain to form a crusty barrier. It is advisable to fork over the mulch two or three times throughout the year to help keep the surface open.

Many local authorities now make their own greenwaste and, although this will be a variable product, it is worth checking out and usually inexpensive.

Potting Composts

Over the years I've had to learn about growing buddlejas in pots and have tried many different types of potting composts. Personally, I prefer not to use peat-based products for buddlejas. When peat compost dries out, it is difficult to evenly rewet, even with wetting agents added. Buddlejas are very hungry feeders, and loam-based composts hold onto fertilizers and trace elements essential for successful development far more efficiently than composts based on peat. In addition, loam-based compost is easier to knock out of the pot when it comes to planting out or repotting. Loam-based composts are heavier than peat-based composts, giving the plant better stability when grown outside. Overall I have had the best results from using a loam-based compost or hardy ornamental nursery stock potting compost with slow-release fertilizer added in the form of pellets coated with a polymer, which will only release the nutrients under the right temperature and moisture conditions in the potting medium. This formulation cuts down nutrient loss through leaching and does not encourage plants to produce soft leafy growth. Buddlejas are very heavy feeders, and unless well fed they will soon become leggy and woody. By transferring young rooted plants in 9-cm (3.5-in) pots directly into 3-L (1-gal) pots of hardy ornamental nursery stock potting compost, they made superb saleable plants within five to six weeks during the main growing season. Large specimen plants should be grown in a pot that is at least 15 L (5 gal) and brought into the glasshouse for winter.

Peat-free compost

Peat resources in the U.K. and parts of Europe are becoming threatened with extinction due to overharvesting. Only about 10 per cent of the peat harvested in Europe is used in the horticultural industry, however, with the bulk being burned as fuel, primarily in Ireland. The National Trust and the Royal Botanic Gardens at Kew and Edinburgh all have adopted a peat-free policy throughout their establishments, and the horticulture industry has been looking for suitable alternatives. The best of them are described here.

Until recently peat-free composts were a real mixed lot due to the variability and inconsistency of the material chosen. The majority of manufactured peat-free composts contain either coir or composted pine bark and loam. Coir is the thick layer of fibre surrounding a coconut. The fibre is strong, durable, and long lasting, in some respects longer lasting than the toughest of peat fibres. Coir was very much a hit-or-miss product in the early years of development and had all sorts of problems associated with it. The first problem to overcome was the major health risks associated with contamination from monkeys defecating in the coir while it was being stored in the country of origin. Because monkeys are very closely related to humans, we share similar diseases, which posed serious risks to gardeners. In addition to solving the monkey problem through better storage methods, screening, grading, and composting processes have come a long way since the early days and much more consistent, uniform products are now available.

Peat-reduced compost

For the fifteen years I was manager and curator at Longstock, we used a peat-reduced compost for our buddlejas and other nursery stock with great success. The compost contained 3 parts peat, 4 parts composted bark chips, 3 parts loam, and 2 parts gravel plus a balanced slow-release fertilizer and magnesium limestone. The usual level of peat was reduced by at least 30 per cent and the amount is made up by the addition of more composted bark. Gravel provides stability, and loam is a good source of trace elements.

Loam-based compost

The majority of loam-based compost mixtures are based on the work done by the John Innes Horticultural Research Institute. These composts are traditionally made with screened and sterilized composted turf, known as loam. Loam has a larger reserve of nutrients and far more trace elements than any other compost ingredient. Although many people think it to be one of those magical ingredients created by the head gardener as a well-kept secret, in fact the process could not be simpler.

Turf is cut from a piece of land that has been kept mown for at least two seasons as lawn. This is where the hire of a turf lifter comes in handy, and it is money well spent. Using the turf lifter, cut the grass roots 1.5 cm (0.38 in) thick and 25 cm (10 in) across in one continues strip. With a half-moon iron, cut across the strip at 1-m lengths and roll into rounds. Lay the strips upside down layer upon layer, much the same way that a lasagne is made, interspersing with bricks and building to a height of about 1.0–1.5 m (3–5 ft). The stack is then left for a minimum of one year and watered regularly. When the stack sags in the middle, it is ready to use. Traditionally the loam is cut from the stack with a spade and sieved through a 5-mm (0.25-in) riddle prior to mixing. The loam may be sterilized in small batches in an oven set to 150°C (325°F); the material should be heated for about fifteen minutes or until it is dry throughout.

John Innes potting composts

I am still amazed how few people understand these wonderful composts to their full potential. John Innes was a property and land dealer in London. Upon his death in 1904, he bequeathed his fortune and estate to the general improvement and development of horticulture through experiment and research. The work of the John Innes Horticultural Research Institute includes standardizing the quantities, ingredients, and methodology of potting compost. At the time, few gardeners understood the importance of sterilizing ingredients to control insects, disease, and weeds or the amount of fertilizers required by each species. After six long years of research and development, the institute's William Lawrence and John Newell determined the physical properties and nutrition necessary to achieve optimum and acceptable plant growth. The results were the famous John Innes seed compost and John Innes potting compost nos. 1, 2, and 3. The institute also developed several heat treatments for sterilizing and pasteurizing loam to eliminate pests, diseases, and weed seeds.

The formula of the John Innes fertilizer (known as base fertilizer) was developed to give a potted plant the best start in its new home for the first two to three months. It contains nitrogen for foliar top growth, phosphates for root development, potash essential for flower and fruit production, and trace elements essential for well-balanced overall plant growth. All of the John Innes composts contain 7 parts sterilized loam, 3 parts peat, and 2 parts washed sharp sand and/or grit (>3 mm, 0.1 in). In addition to these components, for every 36 L of John Innes potting compost no. 1, 100 g (4 oz) base fertilizer and 25 g (1 oz) magnesium limestone are added. For John Innes potting compost no. 2, the amount of base fertilizer and magnesium limestone is doubled; it is trebled for John Innes potting compost no. 3. John Innes seed compost, which has no base fertilizer, is used to sow and germinate seeds and can be used for softwood cuttings.

The main qualities of the ingredients are very important. Loam is the most essential ingredient, as it forms the main body of the compost and is made from natural soils in which a plant would live in the wild. Loam provides essential trace elements such as boron, selenium, zinc, manganese, and sulphur, all vital for quality plant growth and development. Loam also contains clay, which has important cationic and anionic exchange qualities for holding and releasing nutrients as required by the plant. The organic content of the loam helps with water retention and slow release of nitrogen. Water penetration after a plant has dried out is fast and efficient in loam. The best peat for John Innes compost is sphagnum moss peat, which provides improved aeration and water-retaining capacity. The relatively large particle size of sand and grit is important as it helps to keep the compost open. In addition, the weight of sand and grit gives the compost stability and helps prevent larger potted plants from falling over.

Loam- and peat-free nursery stock compost

For those gardeners and nurserymen concerned about the weight of loam-based composts or the environmental degradation associated with peat extraction, a biodegradable foam has been developed for nursery stock compost. This foam replaces loam, making the overall weight a fraction of the traditional mix. The foam's good water retention makes water management very easy. The compost was developed during the National Trust trials and is available to gardeners through Petersfield Growing Mediums of Leicester, as well as other compost manufacturers.

Crushed brick mix

This mixture is very good for those species native to the hottest and driest places, such as *Buddleja utahensis* and *Buddleja marrubiifolia*. I helped develop this mixture while I was at the Royal Botanic Garden, Edinburgh, for the endangered Hawaiian silversword (*Argyroxiphium sandwicense*). After successfully germinating some of the first sowings from the seed batch, we quickly killed them all off after they were potted. Hours of thumbing through the extensive library at Edinburgh led me to the answer. The plant manages to survive among the porous volcanic ash on the side of the sun-baked slopes of the volcano Haleakala on Maui. This black pumice stone was the answer. When trying to find a substitute for the porous volcanic rock, I struck upon the idea that common house bricks were porous and that during manufacture had been exposed to high temperatures. After a quick visit to the rubble yard, I loaded up with the most porous bricks I could put my hands on. I crushed them with a sledgehammer to a pile of dusty crumb-sized pieces and made the first brick mix compost: 70 per cent crushed brick, 15 per cent loam or John Innes no. 1, 15 per cent peat, and a small amount of chelated trace elements. No other fertilizers were used. The silverswords went on to produce the most amazing silvery grey spikes with yellow flowers followed by huge quantities of lovely viable seed, later to be reinstated on Hawaii. The plant has been taken off the endangered species list, and once again it grows in its natural habitat on the volcanic slopes of Haleakala.

Feeding

When buddlejas are fed, the plants bear better and larger blooms, the overall size of foliage increases, and growth is half again as tall. When choosing a fertilizer, consider why you are growing a particular species of *Buddleja*. If it is mostly for their long, scented flowers and attracting butterflies into the garden, a fertilizer high in potash should be used. Buddlejas such as *Buddleja nivea*, *B. loricata*, *B. agathosma*, and *B. indica* are grown mainly for their foliage, which requires nitrogen. Once the reason for growing a particular species is established, selecting a fertilizer suitable to promote either flower or foliage should be straightforward. For optimum flowers, something like a rose or tomato fertilizer high in potassium would be a good choice, for example, 10:15:10 N:P:K. For the best foliage, fertilizer with a high proportion of nitrogen should be applied, for example, 15:10:10 N:P:K.

In early spring the open-ground buddleja collection at Longstock is fed with a general fertilizer with extra potash and top-dressed with composted wood chippings. Always read the package instructions, and never overdose the plant with fertilizer. Too much at one time can kill a plant very quickly, and the best policy is to halve the dosage rate and apply a second application later in the season. When I was an apprentice in the City of Glasgow Parks and Recreation Department, we used to put a thick ring of the blackest and finest well-rotted cow manure around the main root plate of each buddleja along with a couple of handfuls of fertilizer, all watered in well, for the first three to four weeks of the growing season. The results were seen during the late summer, when the blooms were over 25 cm (10 in) long and very sweetly scented.

We grow half-hardy and tender species, such as *Buddleja officinalis* and *B. indica*, in large pots (minimum 25 L) in our own nursery stock compost containing peat, composted bark, sand, grit, base fertilizer, a vine weevil control, and slow-release fertilizer. These plants are overwintered under glass; in spring, when new growth resumes, a top-dressing of general fertilizer is worked into the top layer of soil and fresh potting compost added to bring the level up to the correct height. Prior to the flowers forming, usually in late spring, one to three slow-release fertilizer tablets are pushed into the compost a couple of inches. Because buddlejas are such hungry feeders, I do not like to keep specimen plants in pots for more than a couple of years, as they soon loose their vigour and become woody and misshapen through pruning.

Pruning

Generally speaking the hardy, showy-flowering *Buddleja* hybrids of *B. davidii* respond well to heavy pruning. I prefer to reduce the overall size of the shrub by about one-third before the winter winds blow hard and cold. Doing this helps reduce the amount of resistance by the shrub's foliage as well as the amount of wind rock to the plant. Wind rock weakens or breaks vital root connections and opens up an empty collar around the main stem and the soil or compost, which can fill with water and freeze, thereby killing the plant. Once autumn pruning has been done, it is wise to build up the top-dressing of mulch, as the extra inch or two will give extra root protection against the winters frosts. In late winter or early spring, when young shoots appear and start to break, it is the time to undertake the main pruning and cutting down of the buddlejas. I prune buddlejas in the same way as I would hybrid tea roses, that is, with a good hard pruning—sometimes so hard that people are aghast at what I do. I remove all of the previous year's growth right down to 15–23 cm (6–9 in) from the ground.

A few evergreen species require little or no pruning at all. All that is needed for *Buddleja loricata*, *B. saligna*, *B. coriacea*, and *B. indica* is to prune to shape and deadhead if required. If the plant becomes ugly through old age, however, it will generally respond to the heavy pruning described above, and will break from dormant buds in old wood. I found this out when I butchered a very old *B. saligna* with spectacular results. For the larger, more vigorous species like *Buddleja globosa* and its cultivars, and its smaller cousin *B. nappii*, it pays to show them from time to time whose garden it is and to bring plants under control, cutting the stems back hard. Because they flower early for buddlejas, I favour pruning them directly after flowering. If pruning is left until autumn, there is often extensive dieback and the plant will look unsightly for a long time—possibly up to two years—until it recovers.

Winter-flowering species and hybrids, such as *Buddleja officinalis*, *B. paniculata*, and *B. 'Blue Gown'*, vary in the amount of pruning required. Generally speaking, if they are strong vigorous plants, then they should be pruned hard, down to about 23 cm (9 in), after they have finished flowering.

Deadheading

As with many other plants, *Buddleja* species respond to being deadheaded with a second or third flush of flowers, though these are always much smaller than the main first flush. The other reason for deadheading is a practical one: to avoid self-sown seedlings from germinating all over the place, especially on roofs, chimney breasts, gutters, and other unexpected inaccessible places. It only takes a few minutes to cut off the old flowerheads and pop them into a bucket or barrow. I cut to the second leaf axil from the flower spike, removing the old spent head in one cut. Some flower spikes have small secondary flower panicles at the leaf axils, and I leave these to develop and flower. Secondary flower spikes may have already started to form from the side shoots, and by removing the old head we are releasing the vital nutrients to make more flowers rather than seed.

Removing bark

If your garden is host to the vine weevil, the loose peeling bark of an old or mature buddleja plant is a perfect place for the adult weevils to overwinter. During late summer or early autumn, I always peel away this loose bark just to foil and deprive the weevil of a snug place to overwinter. Be careful that you do not peel away too much, as the plant relies on it for frost protection. Only remove the large, loose pieces.

Watering

The single most important requirement for growing healthy buddlejas is to provide them free-draining soil or compost. Generally speaking, buddlejas are found growing in the wild along gravelly and rocky stream banks or in poor soil at forest edges and clearings. These soils are always free draining and have poor nutrient retention. The desert natives, namely *Buddleja utahensis* and *B. marrubiifolia*, require very little water.

Along with the safe use and disposal of pesticides, governments around the world are imposing regulations on water use. The commercial extraction of water is actively discouraged in the United Kingdom, and hefty fines or imprisonment can be enforced upon the guilty. Nurseries of all sizes must have a reservoir to hold enough water to supply them throughout the summer. The filling of the reservoir must be complete before April and not topped up before November. In the near future, the U.K. government will enforce such water regulations on small private gardens open to the public. When water is stored for any length of time and in volume, however, water-borne diseases such as *Phytophthera* and *Pythium* breed quickly and can be major problem as they are spread around during irrigation. Below I describe several low-tech and inexpensive systems for cleaning water.

Slow sand filter

Although this system is heralded as a new cutting-edge technology, this technique was used in the Victorian period to purify public drinking water. The slow sand filter system proved very effective at reducing and controlling water-borne human diseases such as cholera and typhoid. Municipalities passed reservoir water through huge beds of sand to filter out impurities. They did not know, however, that held within the upper layer of sand there was a *Bacillus* culture which attacked and killed those diseases as a beneficial side effect. This system faded into history as the volume of water to be processed increased. An alternative faster disease-control agent was needed, and chlorine fitted the bill. Many plant diseases such as *Pythium* and *Phytophthera* do not affect people, and in some ways the water quality for human consumption is less critical than that required for plants, particularly at propagation stages.

Construction of a sand filter requires sharp sand to a minimum depth of 1 m (3 ft) over 1 m of 10-mm (0.33 in) pea gravel. These layers need to be free draining and lime free. Rainwater is pumped from the reservoir, passing through a series of various-sized mesh filters to clean the water of debris. From the filters it passes into the top of the sand filter through a sprinkler bar to aerate the water prior to filtration through the sand. This aeration of the water at this stage is very important, as it aids the development of the aerobic *Bacillus* culture, which needs oxygen to work well. Cleaned water is then stored in the main tank from which the irrigation system is drawn. Depending on the temperature, the *Bacillus* culture takes two to four weeks to attain maximum growth for control and will last up to four months before the culture becomes clogged with debris. When this happens, the system is drained and the top 3–4 mm (0.12 in) of sand is removed.

The *Bacillus* culture fights off fungal diseases. This culture is passed on to the plants, and the more they are watered the greater the disease protection.

Treated plants are proving to be resistant to various fungal diseases, and early trials have shown them to have an improved root system as well. The slow sand filter system has another beneficial effect: when the holding tank is full the overflow water is returned to the reservoir, carrying the beneficial bacteria to colonize the water. During the summer, this excess water helps clear the reservoir of algal blooms and control blanket weed.

Capillary sand beds

Capillary sand beds were introduced into nurseries in the early 1980s. Around the time of their introduction, I remember talking to a lot of sceptics who said that the system would not work and plant disease would spread through the crop like a dose of salts. I have never experienced any major disease in the capillary sand bed system. A *Bacillus* culture develops naturally and is held within the sand, and plants grown on the sand bed are inoculated against disease while growing there. Our plants grown on the sand beds always look and grow better compared to similar crops grown on traditional growing beds with overhead irrigation. Plants grown on a sand bed reach a saleable size three to four weeks earlier than in traditional systems. Sand beds are expensive to construct and install, but once set up and running they do produce a very high quality plant and must be considered when funds allow. Beds are constructed outdoors in a similar way to a shallow rectangular pond, with a waterproofed retaining wall and base. The bed is filled with sand, such as washed builder's sand, to a depth sufficient to cover perforated drainage pipes laid to run the length of the sand bed and into a cistern. The water level is controlled by a ball stopcock with an overflow similar to that in a domestic water closet.

Flood bed

This is the poor man's (or home gardener's) capillary sand bed. A flood bed is cost effective to construct on a sloping site. Basically, a shallow rectangular bed is excavated and edged with boards. Plastic sheeting is laid down on the soil surface and secured to the back of the boards. The plastic sheet is covered with 5–8 cm (2–3 in) of open sharp sand, such as washed builder's sand, and the potted plants are placed on top of the sand. Once or twice a week the whole bed is flooded using a seep hose or perforated hosepipe and the plants are watered through capillary action, pulling up the water through the sand into the compost. The system must be allowed to drain completely between floodings.

Recycled runoff water

According to U.K. government regulations, wastewater runoff and storm water will soon be required to be recycled back into nurseries' reservoirs. Water can be collected from roof gutters as well as runoff from the garden, all of which can be collected, channelled, and then piped or pumped into holding tanks, reservoirs, or ponds for use throughout the year. This practice is already in place in several countries in the world. I saw a superb system in Texas, at Haynes Nursery, where every drop of water was accounted for and recycled. To aid the cleaning of this raw water and to reduce the amount of nitrates, many nurseries are now using floating rafts of aquatic plants such as irises, typha, and phragmites.

Winter Protection

Winter weather conditions vary from one part of the world to another and from year to year. Basically, *Buddleja* can be split into four categories with regard to winter protection. Hardy types, such as *B. davidii*, *B. fallowiana*, and *B. globosa*, can withstand all sorts of winter conditions. Root-hardy types, such as *B. crispa*, *B. forrestii*, and *B. lindleyana*, die back with winter frosts and grow again from rootstock each spring; such plants benefit from a deep, free-draining mulch to give extra protection to the roots. Tender types, such as *B. officinalis* and *B. paniculata*, are killed by frosts and should be brought into a frost-free (3–5°C, 35–40°F) glasshouse before the first frosts of winter. Semi-tropical types, such as *B. indica*, can be grown outside in pots during the warmer summer months and brought into a warm glasshouse for the winter.

Wind

During frosty weather, wind is one of the biggest killers of plants as the frozen ground stops roots from sucking up water and the wind desiccates the aerial portion. When the plants dry out, the damage is done. The most natural way to slow down damaging winds is to create a living windbreak.

Such shelterbelt plantings often are planted long before the first development of any garden.

Netting is sometimes overlooked as beneficial for a garden. As much as 50 per cent of the force of wind can be diverted by using some form of netting or webbing. Shelter is achieved for three times the netting height, so a barrier 3 m high will give 50 per cent reduction of the force of the wind 9 m away.

A windbreak screen can be erected around the specimen. Simple stakes are driven into the surrounding ground and hessian or burlap is then wired to the stakes and anchored well. Horticultural fleece can be used in a similar way; I think that it is too white, however, and prefer the natural tones of hessian and burlap. Windbreaks should be placed around plants in midautumn and removed in midspring.

Bubble wrap, a double-skinned layer of polythene with air bubbles trapped between the layers, is a very efficient way of adding frost protection to plants. Again, however, I do not like the look of it, as it reminds me of litter and detracts from the natural look of the garden. I use it only as an extra lining in the glasshouse for winter insulation.

Root mulch

This is a very useful way of giving the root-hardy types and those buddlejas that form a shallow fibrous root pan extra protection without making it look as if the waste removal people are about to go off with your prize plants. The main quality when selecting root mulch is that it must be free draining and have small air pockets, yet not get blown away. Cover the root plate and surrounding soil with a layer of at least 5 cm (2 in). Rough chipped conifer bark, wood chips, seaweed, dry bracken, pine needles, and sweet chestnut shells and husks all make good inexpensive mulch for winter root protection.

Frost protection

Stem splitting is one of the biggest killers of woody plants. In very cold weather, the sap freezes and swells, splitting the bark and often lifting all the bark away from the plants' essential conductive vessels and cambium. Like a frozen water pipe, the liquid is not transferred to the required places as it leaks everywhere.

If bark splitting is common in your garden, it may be worth considering using water pipe lagging. This is a very effective method to help give extra protection against penetrating frosts to the main stems. If done neatly, there is no reason why the lagging should not remain on the plant from midautumn to midspring. Several off-the-shelf products are available through home improvement centres and builders' suppliers. The traditional material is bands of underfelt which is wrapped round and round in a spiral up the stem. A more modern material is closed cell expanded polyurethane foam, preformed to easily slip over water pipes (or plant stems) of various diameters and cut to length with a sharp knife.

Winter watering of pot-grown buddlejas

To achieve good overwintering results, reduce the amount of watering and try to keep the compost on the dry side. One would think watering would be second nature to gardeners, but the correct amount of water for each plant and species is difficult to deliver consistently. If watered too little, the plant will wilt, and too much water will cause nutrient leaching and favourable conditions for liverworts and mosses to establish. When teaching apprentices the understanding behind watering, I explain that we should put ourselves in the place of the plant. We all enjoy having our feet in water during hot dry weather; during the winter, however, it is a miserable experience.

Pests

On the whole buddlejas growing outside are healthy plants and relatively untroubled by pests. Occasionally mammals can prove a problem in the garden locally but none seek out buddlejas in particular. The most likely damage will be from cats using a trunk as a scratching post or grey squirrels in spring peeling bark from the main stems. Mites and insects pose more of a problem.

Damage from insects, mites and other small pests is caused by their chewing, biting, sucking, or tunnelling during feeding. Leafcutter bees, vine weevils, caterpillars, and earwigs feed by biting or chewing pieces of plant tissue with their mandibles. Red spider mites and thrips suck sap from the under surface of the leaf, causing the cells to die and take on a mottled yellow-brown colour. The queen of sucking insects is the aphid, with its long hollow needle-like mouth parts which are inserted through the leaf or stem surface to suck up the plant's sap. Eelworms spend most of their lives inside buds and leaf tissue, causing plant tissue to become twisted and deformed and making the plant unsightly.

Eelworms

Although the common name of the chrysanthemum eelworm (*Aphelenchoides ritzemabosi*) suggests that it is specific to the genus *Chrysanthemum*, the reality is far from that. This pest is happy living in plants such as asters, black currants, Japanese anemones, lavenders, phlox, penstemons, peonies, saintpaulias, strawberries, verbenas, and wallflowers, to name but a few. In the United States and Europe *A. ritzemabosi* has become a significant pest of buddleja, and much breeding and research is being carried out to find cures. In North Carolina, Michael Dirr is experimenting with several new hybrids he has raised; hybrids showing the most resistance to eelworm are *Buddleja lindleyana* crosses.

Eelworm is a particularly nasty pest which can cause a lot of unsightly damage. The main symptoms in buddleja are limp, distorted, and discoloured leaves and damaged or dead leaf buds. During bad infestations the branch tips may look as if the plant has been sprayed with a selective weed killer, twisting and distorting new soft growths. The symptoms are usually present during cool wet summers or during autumn. Flowering is also badly affected, with the inflorescences being small with many dead flowers.

This pest breeds, lives, and feeds on *Buddleja* buds, but can also develop inside the expanded leaves. They only survive externally during prolonged warm wet weather. Eelworms are mobile in water; during periods of prolonged rain or dew they swim over the leaf surface and can be carried in the runoff, spreading very quickly. They usually travel upwards, up to 5 cm (2 in) a night, invading buds and healthy leaves by entering the open stomata. They can also survive in dead or dying host material for up to three to four months.

To identify this pest take a leaf or shoot tip you suspect is infested with eelworm and tear it in small pieces. Place the material in a small clear glass jar half filled with water and leave for an hour. The eelworms wriggle out of the leaf and fall to the bottom of the glass, where they can be seen as a wriggling mass at the bottom. A 10× optical lens will be useful here. There may be leaf hairs among the debris, so look for movement.

The most effective way of avoiding eelworms in a garden is not to introduce them in the first place. This is easier said than done. A good practice is to hold new introductions in quarantine in an area separate from the main garden. If this is not possible, scrutinize all plant material selected prior to leaving the nursery or garden centre. It is also important to check through the rest of the stock on offer; other species may host eelworm, thereby providing a source of infestation. There are no pesticides available to amateur gardeners for the control of eelworms. The only remedy is to destroy affected plants and replace with clean stock.

It is important to keep the area around buddlejas free from weed hosts of this eelworm. These winter hosts include groundsel (*Senecio vulgaris*), sow thistle (*Sonchus oleraceus*), chickweed (*Stellaria media*), goose grass (*Galium aparine*), buttercups (*Ranunculus* spp.), nettles (*Urtica dioica*), and speedwells (*Veronica* spp.). By removing them, one more source of infestation is eliminated. The average home compost heap rarely reaches a sufficiently high temperature to give effective control of this pest. Collect all leaves which drop in the autumn and take them to a recycling centre or dump in a designated green waste centre. Burning is another option, but do check if garden bonfires are allowed in your area. Also, be aware that hedgehogs and other species shelter in piles of woody debris. If a pile has been left standing for any length of time, check it before you burn it.

Eelworms can be killed by raising the temperature of the plant to just below that which would damage the plant cells. Chrysanthemum growers employ a heat treatment whereby the dormant stools are immersed in hot water (46°C, 115°F) for five minutes prior to the cuttings being produced. The stools are plunged into cold water to cool off, and later clean cuttings can be taken as normal and inserted into the rooting medium. This system also works reasonably well with buddleja cuttings, but a longer treatment at a lower temperature is advisable. Plunge the material into water at 43.5°C (110°F) for twenty minutes.

Weevils

Factors affecting the dispersal of pests such as vine weevil are ease of travel by land, air, and sea and the increased use of mail-order nurseries and suppliers. Not all nurseries are as committed as others when it comes to pest control. Vine weevil is one of the major pests in nurseries and gardens alike. I would doubt that there is a garden in Britain that does not have a colony or two lurking in dark corners.

Male vine weevils are in very short supply, and females are able to reproduce by parthenogenesis, a form of cloning. Females lay eggs in soil near the roots of host plants or in the compost of potted plants. Buddleja is just one of their victims, and vine weevils' preferred host plants are almost any plant grown in a container. Many of the eggs laid fail to hatch, but the sheer numbers from one female can quickly start a very strong colony. The larval stage feasts upon the roots of a large variety of host plants. The flightless adult weevils feast upon the leaves and young shoots, climbing up the main stem during the cover of darkness, when they can be found by torchlight. Adult vine weevils eat irregular notches in the leaf margins of many plants. Traps are a good way of checking how bad the infestation is. These are very simple to put in place and can be as simple as crumpled pieces of cardboard. The weevils hide in the folds of the cardboard; check for their presence during the day. Reputable commercial nurseries will take steps to control vine weevil infestations. Until 1990 it was standard to incorporate a persistent organochloride insecticide into hardy ornamental potting compost, and every plant potted on the nursery had protection against the weevil. Then these substances were outlawed and withdrawn from use, leaving the industry wide open to weevil attack. For five or six years the industry floundered to find a suitable, effective, inexpensive control. There are now alternative chemicals and biological controls that will prevent damaging infestations of vine weevil larvae. Gardeners can treat cuttings and container-grown plants with thiacloprid or imidacloprid to protect them against the larvae.

Birds, frogs, shrews, hedgehogs, ground beetles, rove beetles, and some solitary wasps are natural predators of vine weevils. The microscopic pathogenic nematode *Steinernema kraussei* is a native species present in soils throughout Britain. The nematodes enter the vine weevil larvae and infect them with deadly bacteria; within two to three days the larvae turn brown and die. At the nursery we performed a one-year trial using these nematodes as a form of biological control. We found that severe attacks could be warded off only if the nematodes were present in very high numbers. The main drawback is that the nematodes are sensitive to temperature fluctuations; when confined to pots they die when soil temperatures fall below 5°C (40°F) or over 20°C (70°F). The most effective time to apply the nematodes is from late summer to early autumn, when most of the eggs laid during the summer will have hatched but before the grubs are big enough to cause serious damage.

Because adult vine weevils are nocturnal, it is worth going out at night with a torch to look for them on plants. On a small scale, hand-picking is effective. If there are many adults, putting a sheet or upturned umbrella under the plant and shaking vigorously should dislodge them. Collect and destroy them all. Gardeners may also set traps of grease bands or a special glue to trap insects around plants so that the adults become stuck. Check traps first thing in the morning and pick off the weevils.

Figwort weevils (*Cionus scrophulariae*) can sometimes attack buddleja as well. The adults are small (4 mm, 0.16 in) squat weevils. The legless slug-like larvae feed on the foliage, leaving cleanly cut holes. Control figwort weevils with a contact insecticide as soon as damage is seen.

Capsid bugs

Capsid bugs (*Lygocoris pabulinus*) are small insects active during late spring and early summer. Females lay eggs in young twigs of hawthorn, apple, currants, buddleja, and other woody plants. The eggs overwinter on or in woody twigs and buds, hatching in the spring so nymphs are ready to eat the new soft growth. Adults have partly hardened forewings, membranous hindwings, long legs, antennae, and a proboscis. They are bright green or brown and up to 6 mm (0.25 in) long. Nymphs are yellowish green and feed on a wide range of woody plants, changing over to herbaceous perennials during the summer months prior to entering the adult stage. Both adults and nymphs feed on plant tissue by inserting their mouthparts through the epidermis, injecting digestive juices, and feeding on sap. The damage appears as small ragged holes on new soft growths including buds and shoots, then the characteristic tattering follows. During heavy infestations, leaf, bud, and flower growth might be badly deformed or even die off.

Capsid bugs are very elusive; if approached they will quickly drop to the ground or fly away. With careful examination, however, they might be detected. Because of this elusive nature, capsids are difficult to treat, and often the damage has happened before you can notice the browning tissue on the plant. The best control can be achieved by preventative methods, combining both cultural and chemical controls. During autumn and winter, remove all leaves and debris from under plants and nearby hedges and shrubs. Good control can be achieved using a systemic insecticide. Once sprayed on to the leaf surface, the insecticide is absorbed into the plant's sap. When insects attack the plant, the sap is already loaded with the pesticide. This is the most reliable form of control for sap-feeding insect pests.

Caterpillars

Buddleja are known as butterfly bushes, and visits from these colourful visitors delight gardeners the world over. However, the caterpillars of some moths are actually pests of buddleja, causing damage when they eat the foliage.

The caterpillars of vapourer moths (*Orgyria antiqua*) are up to 25 mm (1 in) long. They are grey and marked with red dots and have four tufts of yellow hairs that may cause skin irritations. The caterpillars have evolved these hairs as a way to prevent predation by birds, small mammals, and other predators. From late spring onwards, eggs hatch and the caterpillars feed on the shoots and leaves of buddleja, and many other shrubs and trees, until mid to late summer, when they construct cocoons to pupate in. The flightless females emerge from late summer to early autumn and mate with the winged males. Females then lay 200–300 eggs each on or near their cocoons attached to twigs and branches, and the eggs overwinter. Outbreaks of this pest are usually local and damage is seldom severe; they are most troublesome in urban and suburban gardens.

If a small infestation of vapourer moths arises, remove and destroy eggs, cocoons, and caterpillars; to be safe, wear rubber gloves when picking and handling the caterpillars. One of the easiest and most effective methods I have found is to prune summer-flowering buddlejas in late winter to early spring, depending on the weather, and then burn the prunings or take them to the a local recycling centre. Alternatively use a contact pesticide in spring and summer, when the young caterpillars are active.

The moth pest most frequently encountered on buddlejas in Britain is the mullein moth (*Cucullia verbasci*), which also feeds on *Verbascum* species. The caterpillars are up to 48 mm (2 in) long, greyish white with distinct black and yellow blotches. It is an occasional pest and is often dealt with by hand picking the very distinctive caterpillars during early to midsummer.

In the United States the caterpillars of checkerspot butterfly (*Euphydryas chalcedone*) have been reported feeding on the young foliage of buddleja. The caterpillars are large and bluish black. In Connecticut they advocate the use of the biological control agent *Bacillus thuringiensis* var. *kurstaki*, which is best applied while the caterpillars are small.

Aphids

Aphids are an infrequent pest on garden buddlejas. They damage the host plant by sucking out its juices and injecting toxins into the leaf through a tube-shaped mouth structure called a stylet. These chemicals start the digestion process and act as an anticoagulant, stopping the sap from crusting over. If unchecked, these toxins will distort and twist the leaf, often leading to them drying out and defoliating. Both adults and nymphs feed at the same time, consuming vast quantities of plant sap. Their excrement is a sticky sugary substance known as honeydew. Several fungi flourish on honeydew, the most common being sooty mould. Some species of ants tend aphid colonies. The ants consume the nutrient-rich honeydew, and the aphids gain a secure grazing area free of other predators and parasites— after all, a division of angry ants is a formidable force to be reckoned with.

Aphids have a very fascinating life cycle. They are supreme at the art of reproduction and carry it out at an unceasing rate during their short lives. The colonies consist of winged and wingless adults. The winged ones are not efficient fliers, but they can be transported by the wind for huge distances. Reproduction is mainly asexual, and most aphids are parthenogenetic females. They give birth to live young, miniature copies of themselves, thereby wasting no time in the egg stage. In the autumn, in some aphid species, some of the population will migrate to other winter host plants where they reproduce sexually, and lay overwintering eggs. When temperatures are high enough in spring the newborn aphids will mature and produce young within seven or eight days. Thus, a small aphid infestation can quickly get out of hand.

The secret to controlling aphids is anticipating when to expect the first attack, as well as looking carefully for the first signs of an attack. Keeping notes in a diary from one year to the next will help you to anticipate problems. Treat the plant before the pest has a real chance to do its worst damage. In addition, by reducing the amount of nitrogenous fertilizer applied, the production of new growth will be slowed and toughened, thus making the plant less attractive to aphids.

Nonchemical controls are seldom effective, but many products are available in garden centres which give excellent control of aphids. There are three types of chemicals to choose from, depending on time of year. A winter plant oil wash, as the name suggests, is applied against aphid eggs during the winter. Natural contact chemicals include rotenone (derris), fatty acids, plant oils, pyrethrum, and synthetic chemicals such as bifenthrin are all very effective. A systemic chemical for spraying on plants is imidacloprid.

The main aphid predators, if they get past the guard of ants, are the adult and larval stages of the ladybird beetles. Each female beetle lays about 20–50 eggs a day and larvae will eat up to 100 aphids a day. Try and encourage populations of ladybirds to establish and flourish in your garden. Larvae of lacewings (*Neuroptera*) are very good predators; not only do they eat aphids, they also control red spider mites and thrips. Hoverflies (*Syrphidae*) and aphid parasitic wasps (*Aphidius colemani*) are also effective means of biological control.

Scale insects

Oleander scale (*Aspidiotus nerii*) is not a common pest of buddleja, although there have been several reports on glasshouse plants. The recommended treatment for scale is imidacloprid applied when scales are seen.

Spider mites

Red spider mites (*Tetranychus urticae*) are smaller than a pinhead; the female is larger than the male, and she measures in at 0.5 mm (0.02 in). Their favourite environments provide prolonged warm dry periods, which are present for most of the year in glasshouses. When overwintering tender buddleja in a heated glasshouse or conservatory, this pest often causes slow progressive damage, often going unnoticed and untreated until the leaves turn a sickly yellowish brown. Leaves first show a very fine light yellow speckling and progressively become discoloured, often getting a metallic sheen if left unchecked. The leaf is killed off and drops. By this stage, the mites have reached epidemic proportions and may be traversing the plant on very fine strands of silk webbing.

This pest thrives in dry hot conditions that last for prolonged periods. A very simple and inexpensive control is to mist down plants with water twice or three times a day, paying particular attention to the under surfaces of leaves. As an apprentice, I inherited a glasshouse of aspidistras completely covered in very fine silvery webbing over the leaves. I removed the dead and dying leaves, washed the other leaves with soft soap, and started a misting programme—four or five times during the summer days, reducing to two or three as the days got shorter. This misting programme broke the spider mite's life cycle and the aspidistras all grew out of the problem. For some of the worst affected plants I took drastic steps and cut off all the foliage. With the misting programme, the plants produced beautiful new leaves and recovered much quicker that the others in the crop.

Not all mites are herbivores and the safest way to control red spider mites is with biological control by the predatory mite *Phytoseiulus persimilis*, which reproduces at twice the rate of *T. urticae* when daytime temperatures are above 20°C (70°F). They are sold by mail order to the commercial growers and gardeners in plastic bottles containing 100–2000 mites, kept in tip-top condition with moist vermiculite and ready to do action upon arrival to the glasshouse. They are simply shaken out and scattered among the crop.

Chemical controls are rotenone (derris) and bifenthrin; the former needs frequent applications and the latter may be ineffective, as resistant strains of the pest are widespread. If the infestation is very severe by late summer, for the sake of the entire collection it may be best to discard and destroy the host plant by burning it before the females find other overwintering sites.

Japanese beetles

Japanese beetles (*Popilla japonica*) are not fussy eaters and will have a go at most buddlejas. The adult beetles are about 10–13 mm (0.4–0.5 in) in length and bright shiny green with copper-coloured wing cases. They have distinctive white markings at the end of their abdomen and five fine white spots on the sides. Japanese beetles appear during early summer and they reach their climax about midsummer. During drought conditions their numbers are greatly reduced. In the United States Japanese beetle traps are readily available from good hardware stores and garden centres. The traps are sticky inside with hug-tight glue and are baited with sex pheromones and some choice plant extracts to draw them into it. It is advisable to site the traps away from the most valued plants in the garden—after all, these traps work the same way as a pub with free beer, and the beetles come from miles around. Because the larvae develop in turf and feed on the root system, it may be worth considering treating the lawn to reduce infestations. Japanese beetles are not a problem in the United Kingdom.

Snails and Slugs

Generally speaking, buddleja are not troubled by snails and slugs as they find the leaf hairs unpalatable and difficult to move over. However, snails and slugs can be a problem during propagation, feeding on the most tender of shoots. Their mouthpieces have a rough tongue (called a radula) covered with thousands of tiny hooks which crunch away at plant tissue.

Both snails and slugs are controlled by the same chemical and physical means. Slug pellets are quick, efficient, and easy to apply. For environmental reasons always buy the blue ones, as birds do not associate the colour blue with food. A liquid formulation is also available and is applied as a drench. One major disadvantage of chemical control is the risks to wildlife, especially thrushes, who sometimes catch a treated snail and consume both snail and poison. Generally speaking, one or two treated snails would not harm an adult thrush, but there is often a glut of snails, and thrushes pick off many at one sitting with tragic consequences. Snails and slugs can be deterred by putting something between the plant and the pests. According to the weather, chimney soot, coal ash and cinders, and copper bands may be effective. Biological control in the form of parasitic nematodes (*Phasmarhabditis hermaphrodita*) is available by mail order. The packs contains millions of microscopic nematodes (eelworms), which you add to water and apply with a watering can during early spring to midautumn. Nematodes will control slugs for up to six weeks.

Biological Pest Control

Predacious insects and mites used in biological control are sold in plastic bottles with fine mesh tops to allow air movement. They are kept in tip-top condition with moist vermiculite and are ready to do action upon arrival in the glasshouse. Speed between dispatch and delivery of the colonies is vital for the success of the whole exercise, as the fresher the colony the better the control. The contents are simply shaken out and scattered among the plants. From there they climb the plants in search of prey. The suppliers assure us in the industry that they do not survive our winter conditions outdoors and that there is little chance of affecting the natural balance of our habitats.

Biological controls give environmentally friendly control of some difficult pests.

Parasitic wasps (*Encarsia formosa*) are commercially available parasites. Several sources make this natural-born killer readily available to both the professional and the amateur alike. The wasps are supplied as pupae on stiff white cards which are hung among the plants. *Encarsia formosa* is only effective in the controlled environment of a glasshouse or conservatory and needs daytime temperatures of 20°C (70°F) and above if it is to breed faster than the pest, although it can survive at lower temperatures.

Several other predatory insects are available through commercial suppliers. *Metaphycus helvolus* is a parasitic wasp that controls soft scale insects in glasshouses. For best results, the wasps should be released in midsummer. The lacewing *Chrysoperla carnea* is a British native species that is also found throughout North America; *C. rufilabris* is found in the more humid regions of the United States. A lacewing larva will eat more than twenty aphids in a single day, making lacewings one of the best controls for this pest. Lacewing eggs can be placed within the garden or crop at the first sign of an aphid infestation, usually early in the season. The two-spot ladybird beetle, *Adalia bipunctata*, is a very common native insect in the United Kingdom. Adult beetles are sold in clear plastic tubes to be released in the garden. Other species of ladybird beetles are commercially available in other parts of the world as well.

Glasshouse red spider mite can be controlled by a predatory mite, *Phytoseiulus persimilis*, which is available by mail order from suppliers of biological controls. Like other predators and parasites, it needs warm daytime conditions, good light intensity, and an absence of pesticide residues. Its season for use is late spring and early autumn.

Organic Pesticides

There are several types of organic chemicals to choose from, depending on the time of year. A winter wash based on plant oils, as the name suggests, is applied during the winter. It is diluted and applied as a drenching spray, paying particular attention to peeling, scaling, and cracked bark and cavities. Owing to the possible scorching and burning properties of the chemical, it can only be used on deciduous woody plants that are fully dormant. It is important not to spray too late in the winter-spring season, as damage to leaves can occur during bud-break. The oil kills off many overwintering insects, such as scale, and eggs of aphids.

Contact organic chemicals, such as rotenone (derris) and pyrethrum, are sold as a concentrate for diluting down or as ready diluted sprays, and are applied to the plant during the growing season. Be careful of beneficial insects, such as bees, and spray either early in the morning before other insects are flying or late in the day after they have settled, usually about an hour before sunset.

Other contact organic chemicals for use on plants in leaf include sprays containing plant oils or fatty acids. Again, be careful of beneficial insects.

Derris is produced by grinding the tubers of a tropical woody plant from the genus *Derris*, and it is one of the safest ways to control red spider mites. The main active substance is a poison called rotenone. This chemical also can be used as a poison to kill fleas, mites, and other parasites on domesticated animals and humans with no negative side effects. For centuries, native peoples have used mashed up derris pulp to poison fish in streams and lakes for consumption. Thus, one must be extremely careful when using this chemical. Do not contaminate watercourses and ponds containing fish, as the slightest bit of derris or any other insecticide will kill fish. In addition, do not use in conservatories where there is a display of fish unless the water surface has been completely covered over.

The source of pyrethrum is the dried flower-heads of *Chrysanthemum cinerariifolium*. Just before they open the flower-heads are collected, completely dried, and then ground into a fine powder. This very effective naturally occurring insecticide can be used either as a dust or as a solution extracted from the dust and applied to the plant as a spray.

Diseases

During the three decades that I have been growing *Buddleja*, I have found the genus to be nearly disease-free. In the nursery, damping off and virus may affect the plants. Thankfully, however, these problems are restricted to the early stages of plant development and should not trouble gardeners.

Damping off

Germinating seeds and seedlings are at most risk of damping off caused by *Pythium* and other fungi. The disease affects most plant species grown from seed. The fungi are water and soil borne and attack the seedling stem at or below soil level. The first sign of the disease is lesions on the stem followed by narrowing or shrivelling. The infected seedling appears wilted, and soon collapses and dies. The most effective control is achieved by applying fungicide at first sign of the disease, using either copper oxychloride or Cheshunt Compound.

Good hygiene and cultural methods are also important in avoiding the disease. Trays, pots, and pans should all be sterilized in a horticultural disinfectant and new fresh compost used. The seeds should be sown thinly and watered with clean or deionized water. Risk of damping off is increased by overcrowded seedlings, by using old or unsterilized compost, and by watering with collected rain water (because Pythium is water borne, water butts are the perfect places for it to establish and breed).

Other conditions that foster damping off include a warm humid atmosphere and little air movement; a small electric fan will improve air circulation if bad weather means the vents cannot be opened. Remove germinating seedlings from the vicinity of other propagation material to prevent cross contamination, and as soon as the seedlings show signs of green shoots take them out of the greenhouse.

Virus

Viruses cause yellow mottling and distortion of the leaves. In severe cases the inflorescence may be stunted and much branched. Infected plants should be destroyed. The two viruses known to affect buddlejas are alfalfa mosaic (AMV) and cucumber mosaic (CMV), and both may be aphid and seed borne. For this reason seed should not be collected from infected plants. Meristem culture can be used to generate virus-free plants commercially.

The Dos and Don'ts of Growing Buddlejas

	Do	Don't
Hardy types USDA zones 5–9	Plant in any free-draining soil	Plant in deep shade, as they will not grow or perform well
	Use a sterile organic mulch around the base, such as wood chips, bark chips, or cocoa shells	Plant in wet soils (this is one sure way to kill buddlejas)
	Plant in full sun or light or semi-shade	Allow wind rock during winter high winds
	Feed in spring with a balanced N:P:K fertilizer	Buy any stock with deformed leader growths (possibly infested with eelworm)
	Prune by half in autumn to reduce root rock	Buy any stock with variegated foliage apart from known forms
	Prune hard in spring to stimulate strong growth and flowers	
	Prune to shape	
	Deadhead the flowers	
Root-hardy types USDA zones 7–9	Try to establish in a sheltered spot in the garden	Plant in cold sites
	Have replacements in reserve	Plant in wet soils
	Plant in a sheltered place in semi-shade in a south-facing spot in a mixed border	Plant in a site exposed to north-easterly wind
	Use a thick layer of chunky mulch , such as coarse chipped bark, around the roots to give extra root protection	Allow wind rock during winter high winds
	Use sterile organic mulch around the base, such as wood chips, bark chips, or cocoa shells	Lift until late spring or early summer as regrowth from roots might occur
	Feed in spring with a balanced N:P:K fertilizer	Buy any stock with deformed leader growths (possibly infested with eelworm)
	Then feed with a high-potash fertilizer six to eight weeks later to encourage flower production	Buy any stock with variegated foliage apart from known forms

Do	Don't	
Prune after flowering if the plant flowers in spring and early summer		**Root-hardy types** USDA zones 7–9 *(continued)*
Prune in spring if it flowers late in the season		
Prune to shape		
Deadhead the flowers		
Use sterile organic mulch around the base, such as wood chips, bark chips, or cocoa shells	Plant in cold sites	**Tender types** USDA zones 9–12
Try to establish in a sheltered spot in the garden	Plant in wet soils	
Prune to shape	Allow wind rock during winter high winds	
Deadhead the flowers	Overwater the plant	
Prune after the plant flowers in the spring or early summer	Put outside if there is risk of frost	
Prune in spring if it flowers in late summer or early autumn	Become upset if once planted out it dies—do keep trying	
Grow in a container and bring into protection before first frost	Buy any stock with deformed leader growths (possibly infested with eelworm)	
Reduce the amount of watering during the winter protection period	Buy any stock with variegated foliage apart from known forms	
Have replacements in reserve		
Feed in spring with a balanced N:P:K fertilizer		
Plant in a sheltered place in semi-shade in a south-facing spot in a mixed border		
Use a thick layer of chunky mulch, such as coarse chipped bark, around roots to give extra root protection		

Chapter 4

Propagation

Most gardeners want to be able to grow their plants from scratch. The reasons for doing your own propagation are many: the challenge of successfully rooting a cutting or germinating a seed, the pride and pleasure of successfully propagating the plant, having specimens of rare plants which are not widely available in commercial nurseries, and saving money. Another reason often overlooked is the friendship, as having plant material to give to fellow gardeners strengthens our bonds with them. The giving and receiving of plant material is an ancient one among gardeners, and you never know when disaster will strike in your garden. Losses are heartbreaking and can be very hard to overcome. To some people, it is sheer madness to give away a rare, unusual, or favourite plant. Over my three decades in gardening, however, this has been a very successful strategy. I have been so glad to retrieve propagation material from friends when my plant had died, was stolen, or was damaged beyond repair.

Propagating from Seed

Growing buddleja from seed is the simplest and least expensive way of raising large numbers of plants. This process is a bit like playing the lottery, however, as you don't know what you have won until the plant flowers. You might have won the top prize of the car, or maybe it is just the bar of soap. Buddlejas are very promiscuous and will cross-pollinate with almost any other buddleja nearby. Together they have an enormous gene pool and vary in size, shape, form, leaf, and flower colour. Sometimes seedlings prove to be throwbacks to previous generations of parents with some very interesting surprises.

Mature seed capsules are usually dry and brown and frequently have the remains of the old flowers attached. The two halves of the capsule split open when mature, usually during hot dry weather, releasing the seed from the capsule walls into the air to be dispersed. Buddlejas have a long flowering and seed-ripening period; to avoid premature seed dispersal, several visits may be required to successfully gather the seeds. Alternatively, a clear plastic bag can be placed over the chosen capsules to collect the ripening seeds. Seed collection should be done during dry weather after midday, when all moisture from the night before has been evaporated by the sun. This will reduce the chance of any fungi, yeasts, and moulds forming on the seeds and pods. Owing to the tiny size of buddleja seed, there is little or no period of dormancy. Thus, the seed can be sown straight away or can be kept in an envelope in a dark, dry, and cool but frost-free place.

Seed collection

The equipment required for seed collection includes basic everyday objects: paper bags and envelopes (even old used envelopes) of different sizes to hold the seed and a waterproof container such as a large plastic bag to carry the filled seed bags and envelopes; a pencil to note what it is in the bag; a small notebook to record field notes; and secateurs, a sharp knife, or even a small craft knife to remove seed capsules from the donor plant.

Vital collection information should be written on the bag or envelope prior to collection of the seed, which makes the task of writing on the bag much easier. It is essential to record the following information: date of collection, location, species, cultivar or hybrid showing the parentage, collector's name, and identification number if one is available. If collecting seed in the wild, it is also useful to record site aspect (for example, south-facing), soil type, elevation, mature size of the parent plant, and weather conditions during collection. An accurate record will prove to be invaluable in years to come. We should not leave these details to our memories, because our memories do fade and plants and collections get handed, replanted, or transplanted over the years.

When collecting seed, it is not essential for the capsules to be totally dry, but they should be dry enough to break away from the main stem under gentle pressure. The capsules can finish ripening in a paper bag or envelope hung in a cool dry room. During collection, the seed capsule should be placed into the bag or envelope prior to it being cut from the plant. By doing it this way, the free-falling seeds—often the most viable seeds in the capsule—can be collected. For larger plants, I suggest holding a large plastic tray, box, or polythene sheet without holes under the seed capsule prior to cutting it off.

Cleaning and storing seed

If a small quantity of seed is to be cleaned, this is best done by shaking the seed heads onto a sheet of white letter-sized paper. Using a stiff short wire, such as a straightened paperclip or a large needle, separate seed from the chaff. A magnifying lens may prove useful at this stage; lenses held in a clamp frame which can be positioned anywhere are sold in most craft stores.

Larger quantities of seed require a range of sieves of various mesh sizes. By working sequentially from the largest to the smallest mesh, most of the chaff can be separated from the seed. Usually at the end of this process there is a mixture of chaff and seed of equal size, and it can be tricky to separate the two. Because the chaff is usually lighter than the seed, however, soft blowing across the sieve will drive the chaff away. When the seed is lighter or the same weight as the chaff, this blowing technique results in seed and chaff everywhere but in the sieve. When cleaning this type of seed, a fine paintbrush is the ideal tool to gently brush the chaff to one side of the sieve and remove it.

The cleaned seed should be stored in a small, dry, carefully labelled envelope folded in such a way that it will not leak the seed. Stamp collectors use semiclear greaseproof envelopes which are ideal for storing cleaned seed, and these can be written on with a pencil. Store seed in a dark, dry, and cool but frost-free place away from mice, ants, woodlice, and silverfish. If the conditions are right, seed can be stored for many years before sowing.

Seed composts

All seeds share the same basic requirements: they need the right temperature, the right amount of moisture, and the right amount of air with humidity. Seed compost must be free-draining yet retain moisture, and it must be porous enough to allow sufficient air to get to the germinating seed. As we all know, mustard, cress, and mung beans can germinate on moist kitchen paper, but they soon run out of nutrients around the development of the first true leaf. Seeds have sufficient nutrient reserves to develop from germination to the first true leaf stage. Thus, germinating seeds are not looking for nutrients.

Although I have tried many of the ready-made seed composts, I have had the best results germinating buddleja seed using good loam-based composts such as John Innes Seed Compost. These loam-based composts can also be easily made at home; with a little practice at mixing and ensuring a clean mixing surface, anyone will have good results. The recipe for a loam-based seed compost mixture is as follows:

> 2.2 L riddled and or sieved peat
> 2.2 L sharp sand (>3 mm, 0.1 in)
> 1.1 L sterilized loam (see chapter 3)
> 30 g (1 oz) of ground limestone
> 1 teaspoon of superphosphate

Sowing

Loosely fill the seed tray flush with the top, and strike off the excess. To compact the compost evenly to the required density, tap the tray 5–8 cm (2–3 in) several times on the work surface. With a flat piece of wood that fits inside the top of the tray or the base of another seed tray, gently press down to flatten the compost surface about 1.3 cm (0.5 in) below the rim. Next place the tray in a basin of water half the depth of the tray and allow it to stand long enough for the compost to become thoroughly wet. Remove the tray from the water and allow it to drain freely for about thirty minutes.

Fill in the uneven hollows and crevices of the compost by sieving fine sand over the surface. My journeyman taught me another valuable trick using sand for sowing fine seeds like those of buddleja. Mix the seeds with a small amount of dry light-coloured sand, thereby giving bulk and a visual marker to aid even sowing. Then divide the seed into two lots. Sow one lot in one direction over the compost and the other lot in the opposite direction. This will help to sow the seed evenly and reduce overcrowding; damping off can arise in overcrowded seed trays.

Record on a label the important details of the seed batch, and push it between the compost and the side of the tray, below the rim. Place a piece of glass snugly over the top of the tray, followed by several layers of newspaper or brown paper to keep out the light. In nurseries, seed trays should be placed in a warm frame with a bottom temperature of 24.5°C (75°F). Likewise, home gardeners should find a place that is consistently warm and dark, such as an airing cupboard or windowsill, or use a propagator with a thermostatically controlled heated base. Avoid large fluctuations in temperatures—too hot will cook the seeds and too cold will rot them. Two weeks prior to sowing the seed, it's a good idea to put a thermometer that records minimum and maximum temperatures where you plan to place the trays.

Check the trays twice a day by removing the paper and gently removing the glass. To prevent drips, avoid tilting the glass until it is clear of the seedlings. Shake off the excess condensation from the glass, replace it upside down, and cover it again with the paper. In glasshouses, keep a look out for cats, mice, slugs, snails, woodlice, and other nuisances that love to mess up our hard work. Continue this process of turning the glass until the first sign of germination; when this happens, the rest of the seedlings will emerge in a day or so.

At the first sign of a green shoot, remove the glass and paper and bring the tray into light, while avoiding full sun. To water the newly germinated seeds, plunge the tray into a basin of water to half the depth of the tray and leave it to soak until dark wet patches appear on the surface. Remove the tray from the basin and allow it to drain thoroughly. Once the seedlings have the first pair of true leaves, they can be watered overhead by a watering can with a fine rose.

At this stage I like to give the seedlings a liquid feed, and I prefer a natural seaweed fertilizer, weakly diluted and applied every second watering. I am a strong believer that if you find a good product and it performs well, then you should stick to it—and I have been using this natural organic and nontoxic product for nearly thirty years. It has several advantages over other liquid fertilizers. Its effect on the plant is instant, as both leaves and roots absorb the nutrients. It is difficult to overdose with and, in my experience, helps to reduce fungal attack such as damping off. It does not harm the environment and, best of all, a little goes a long way, so it is cost effective as well.

Pricking out seedlings

Seeds should be pricked out as early as possible to minimize root damage and speed up development. Many dexterous and experienced people can successfully carry out this task at the seed leaf stage of germination. People's dexterity varies however, and some of us must wait until the seedlings are larger before we handle them. I have only met two people really adept at pricking out seedlings. Perhaps not surprisingly, they both had small hands.

When handling the young seedlings, it is very important not to damage the main stem of the plant. Handling a seedling by the stem will usually crush it, making it vulnerable to disease and causing it to grow poorly and probably die. Over the years I have explained to many apprentices that it is better to damage a leaf, as the plant can recover and grow a new one. Traditionally, seedlings were pricked out into trays and grown on for a season or so. But when time came to pot them on, plants had to be pulled apart from one another, causing considerable root damage. The overcrowded conditions also checked vigorous growth. Over the years, several new products have been devised to minimize root disturbance and prevent overcrowding, including fibre or whale-hide pots, Jiffy 7 pots, peat blocks, paper cells, and rock or glass wool. These pots and materials were planted on with the plant, as the roots were meant to grow through them into the new soil or compost. In reality, however, all of these products had problems, such as the roots not penetrating the media, difficulty in rewetting the material, or insufficient support for the growing shoots.

I favour plastic cell trays for pricking out seedlings. These trays come in various sizes, colours, and number of cells per tray. This system greatly reduces root damage and does not interrupt plant growth after repotting. Each young plant, or plug, can be pushed out from the bottom of the cell, with root system intact and ready to grow into the new potting compost; cone shaped cells mean the plugs can be inserted easily.

Root trainers are also a useful system because their design incorporates grooves the full length of the module, which encourages the roots to grow downwards instead of round and round the pot, thus giving a stronger root system when planted out. The other advantages of root trainers are that they are hinged and separate in two halves so the young plants can be easily removed and that they are made of recyclable plastic, although I manage to reuse them for several seasons. They are ideal for the larger more vigorous species such as *Buddleja globosa*. Root trainers are 8–12 cm (3–4.75 in) deep and the cells are arranged in units of four, six, and eight.

Vegetative Propagation from Cuttings

Good hygiene is essential for successful propagation. When selecting and taking cutting material from the parent plant, it is very important to select only good strong healthy material from a donor plant free of any sign of pests and diseases. Many horticultural pests and diseases are innocuous outdoors; when they are brought into an ideal enclosed environment, however, they can quickly reach epidemic proportions. One of the first principals of successful propagation is the maintenance of a clean disease-free environment. Each day remove any fallen, dead, diseased, or damaged leaves and cuttings, as they provide an ideal breeding ground for diseases such as grey mould (*Botrytis cinerea*).

Professional propagators also sterilize the trays by dipping them in a large container of horticultural disinfectant solution. Once or twice a year the whole propagation house should be washed down, inside and out, with the same solution as used on the trays, paying particular attention to the dark, damp, out-of-the way places, where the bugs hide. In addition, use fresh rooting compost only once and discard it on the compost heap after potting on.

Collecting the plant material

The following tools are required during the collection of material:

    a plastic bag for each variety of gathered material
    a larger black polythene sack to hold the bags of collected cuttings
    a pair of secateurs
    a sharp knife
    a pair of thick leather gloves
    a notebook to record information in the field or garden
    blank labels
    pencils

Several designs of secateurs are available on the market. The parrot-billed scissor type gives a superior clean cutting action, causing little damage to the surrounding tissue in comparison to the anvil (or rollcut) type, which has a blade that crushes the stem, damaging cells and providing an entry point for diseases.

A razor-sharp knife always gives the best results—it is as important as a scalpel to a surgeon. Sharpening a knife is a skill, which can be learned with practice and patience. If you find it difficult or cannot sharpen a knife to razor sharpness, buy an inexpensive disposable craft knife with a snap-off blade. Once it has lost its sharp edge, simply snap off the blunt part to reveal a new razor-sharp cutting edge. To prevent painful cuts and visits to the hospital, it is always advisable to wear leather gloves or a leather thumb stool when using sharp instruments.

Success with cuttings starts with the selection of top-quality material. Young vigorous growths make the best propagation material. Cuttings should be collected, prepared, and inserted in the same day; the shorter the time between collecting and inserting, the better the chances of rooting. The best time to collect the cutting material is first thing in the morning, when the plant has recharged its water levels during the cool of the night and before the sun strikes its surface.

The plant should be turgid. During dry spells, when growth is right for propagating, liberally water the parent plant a day or so prior to collecting the propagation material. Avoid shoots with flower buds, as roots take much longer to initiate and the death of the cutting is common. Cut off the selected shoots with a pair of secateurs, place them in a plastic bag, and close the bag to avoid drying out. Label the cut material, and record the plant name, date and other appropriate field notes.

An overnight or day's delay in inserting the cuttings is sometimes unavoidable, especially when travel is involved. The cutting material still in their plastic collection bags should be stored in a dark cool place. The salad section of the refrigerator is the most suitable place, but it should be no cooler than 2°C (35°F). Alternatively, I have used a cool box in the boot of my car to transport material when visiting gardening friends. When leaving home, place an ice pack in the box to chill it and remove the ice prior to the return journey. I have found that this keeps cuttings almost as fresh, if not fresher, than when they were collected. If you do not have a cool box, wrap the cuttings in wet kitchen paper or newspaper and place them in a plastic bag. This will keep them fresh for twenty-four hours if kept cool. I have brought back several varieties from Europe using this method.

For buddlejas, the best type of cuttings are nodal cuttings. The node is the part of the stem where the leaves are attached; there is often a distinct swelling in this area. Large concentrations of plant growth hormones are produced at the nodes. The trick is not to cut away or through these hormone hot spots. The general rule of thumb for all nodal cuttings is to make one smooth cut 3–7 mm (0.1–0.3 in) below the node at right angles to the main stem.

Compost for cuttings

The main functions of a good propagation compost are to hold the cutting in an upright position while providing contact with moisture and to allow sufficient air into the compost around the base. The compost has to be clean and free from weed seeds and diseases. Cuttings do not have roots, so the compost needs little or no nutrients; it is only after rooting that they require nutrients. Traditional propagation compost is 1 part sieved peat, 1 part washed sharp sand, and no added fertilizer.

Most professional propagators have their own "secret recipe root-all magic compost." These may contain rock wool, bark products, vermiculite, and perlite. I know people who have great success either with sand, bark, or peat alone as a rooting medium. Personally I prefer to use a mix of equal parts composted bark, perlite, and vermiculite. My comments below describing the various components suitable for inclusion in a propagating mix are based purely upon personal experience, training, and theory. Ultimately, it is the quality of the ingredients that is most important.

Many types of sand are available, but very few are of a quality suitable for propagation purposes. To provide the optimum drainage, the sand particles should be of uniform size (3 mm, 0.1 in) and shape, with little or no impurities. Another factor to consider when choosing suitable sand is the pH; buddlejas prefer pH in the range of 5.5 to 8.5. Buy the proper propagation sharp sand from a garden centre—it is worth the extra cost.

Peat is a natural product of decaying vegetable matter from two dominant plant species whose habitats are constantly boggy. Sedge peat is derived from *Carex* species, and sphagnum peat comes from *Sphagnum* moss. The younger peat is sphagnum, and it is extracted from the tops of bogs. Suitable peat should still contain visible and identifiable remnants of the parent plant. Owing to its larger particle size, sphagnum peat is ideal for propagation as it helps maintain the proper moisture-to-air ratio. The peat should be passed through a riddle or sieve (4 mm, 0.16 in) prior to mixing with sand.

Perlite is a very lightweight expanded volcanic rock that is ground to a diameter of 4 mm (0.16 in) and sold commercially. It is available from garden centres and comes in various sizes of bags. Perlite is very good at maintaining a proper moisture-to-air ratio. I recommend keeping unused perlite in a sealed container. When dry this product is difficult to control, especially when it escapes and hides in car carpets; it seems to stay there for an eternity. Perlite can be dusty, so I recommend watering it prior to mixing.

Vermiculite is an industrial by-product. It is a form of the mineral mica which has been expanded through extremes of heat. Vermiculite is a creamy tan colour, with lightweight multilayered particles. Like perlite, it maintains a good moisture-to-air ratio when included in compost mixes. I suggest keeping unused vermiculite in a sealed container as well.

Composted tree bark finally is getting the recognition it deserves. The innovative leaders in the peat-free compost market have raised bark to its proper place in the horticultural industry. It comes in various grades and various stages of composting. A bark-based propagation compost is well worth searching out as a peat substitute. (The bag sizes, however, tend to be aimed at the grower who uses large quantities.) Microorganisms within the composted bark aid rooting and the general health of the young plant.

During the early 1990s I carried out trials at the nursery using rock-wool rooting blocks for propagation. Rock wool is commonly used in the insulation industry and for hydro-culture. In many respects, it was successful. Rooting was good once the watering regime was mastered. Its main drawback, however, was the total lack of support for the neck of the cutting. Unless checked, later in the production process the plants ended up being very floppy.

Rooting aids

Many people use rooting hormone powders and liquids to increase rooting success. There are several products on the market for both the professional and amateur propagator. Some nurseries use liquid solutions of the natural root-inducing hormone indolebutyric acid (IBA). Naphthalenacetic acid (NAA) has also been tried and tested with varying degrees of success. These plant hormones are not available to the general public.

Hormone rooting powder, however, is sold in retail packages aimed at the home gardener. This product is popular owing to its ease of use and long shelf life if kept cool and frost-free. A small quantity should be dispensed into a shallow dish for each propagation session. When finished, discard the unused powder safely per the instructions on the container. Never put it back in the original container. This practice prevents any disease from the plant material contaminating future propagation sessions, and it avoids getting moisture in the system. It also keeps the powder free from unwanted debris and the active chemical in prime condition.

One of the drawbacks of rooting powder is that the hormone is carried in talcum powder for evenness of distribution. If the cutting's end is very wet, however, it may hold too much powder. Once inserted in the compost the excess powder may form a hard crust between the cutting and the compost, resulting in failure. Tapping the cutting on the side of a tray or pot, or with a pencil, after dipping can prevent any excess build-up.

Water

In parts of England limescale deposits are a major problem when using mains water. Over a relatively short time these calcium deposits and other salts build up on the leaf surfaces, reducing their ability to photosynthesize and extending rooting time. In some regions limescale deposits can even be toxic to plants. In such areas, use deionized water, or collect and boil rainwater; raw rainwater is unsuitable for propagation purposes as most likely it will harbour diseases and impurities (see chapter 3).

Insertion of cuttings

Good contact between the compost and cut surface of the cutting is one of the most crucial parts of the propagation process. Often cuttings fail because the cut surface is sitting in a void, not in contact with the compost or moisture. Many people follow the traditional method of firming the compost and using a dibber to make a small hole in the compost prior to insertion of the cutting. After inserting the cutting, the dibber is used to press down on the compost on either side of the stem. This sometimes damages the stem, however, leaving it vulnerable to disease or death. I prefer to fill the tray loosely and strike off the excess compost. I then push the cuttings into the compost to the required depth. After filling the tray with cuttings I water in the cuttings overhead with a watering can with a fine rose. This settles the compost sufficiently to hold the cuttings in place, and it maintains good contact with the compost so capillary action takes over to ensure a moist environment.

Softwood cuttings

I much prefer soft young material for vegetative propagation, as it results in plants with the best structure and shape. The cuttings should be taken early in the season, soon after growth has started and before the stem begins to go woody. Select vigorous turgid new shoots, as this type of material gives the best rooting success.

Once collected, place the cuttings in a plastic bag along with a label. Fold the end several times to seal the bag to prevent water loss. Always keep the collected bags of cutting material in a black polythene sack to minimize photosynthesis and loss of moisture from the propagation material. The main downside of this method is that, due to the softness of the growth, the cutting material wilts rapidly; therefore, it is imperative to process the cuttings quickly. In the nursery, a mist bench in the propagation house is used to keep the cuttings from drying out, and humidity is kept high. The air temperature is kept constant. A propagation house should also have bottom heat over the length and breadth of the benches, which helps to stimulate the rooting hormones into action. Alternatively, if horticultural facilities are limited, the cuttings can be inserted in trays or pots covered with clear plastic sheeting or a clear bag secured with an elastic band or raffia, or stood in a propagating case, preferably with a heated base.

Young vigorous soft shoots have short distances between the nodes. As the cuttings are being prepared, it is always good practice to nip out the top growth point, as this benefits the overall shaping and branch structure of the adult plant. Remove the lower leaves by rubbing them out with your thumb, which encourages secondary rooting up the stem, keeping only two to four upper leaves. Roots will often sprout from the points at which the lower leaves were removed, which aids the rooting process. If the upper leaves are large, such as those of *Buddleja nivea* var. *yunnanensis*, reduce the overall leaf size by cutting it to one-half to one-third of its original size. This will help reduce water loss and aid faster rooting. Some people contend, however, that any damage to the foliage will pave the way for future fungal diseases and say the leaves should be left entire. Over the three decades of my career, I have not noticed this to be true. Good cultural hygiene in the propagation house holds the secret to success.

The ideal cutting length is 10–13 cm (4–5 in). Dip the lower cut end into hormone rooting powder, tap off the excess, and insert the cutting in 1:1 peat and sharp sand mix. Water the cuttings well. If using a mains water, it is advisable to have a reservoir to let the chlorine evaporate before using the water. Chlorine has been blamed by some propagators for reduced rooting percentages of some species and genera, including *Buddleja*. Finally, cover with glass (if in a frame), a propagating case cover, or a plastic bag secured with an elastic band or raffia. The cuttings should root in about ten to fourteen days.

Semi-hardwood cuttings

These cuttings are taken at a slightly later stage of development than softwood cuttings, when the young shoots are starting to thicken up after midsummer. The stem is bendable, as opposed to the softwood cutting which will snap easily. Semi-hardwood, or half-ripened, material has the benefit of being older, so more reserves are held within the cutting to sustain it through the rooting process.

Take cuttings 10–13 cm (4–5 in) long from nonflowering half-ripened shoots during mid to late summer. The same method of cutting preparation as described for softwood cuttings applies to semi-hardwood cuttings. Again, insert the cuttings in a rooting medium such a 1:1 mix of peat and sharp sand, and place them either under a mist unit or lined out in a tightly covered cold frame. Alternatively, they can be inserted in a propagating case or in trays or pots covered with a clear plastic sheeting or a clear bag secured with an elastic band or raffia. Cuttings should root within two to three weeks.

Heel cuttings

A heel cutting is a shoot torn from the main stem with a triangular piece of bark and cambium attached, resembling the heel of a foot. The material that is the heel includes the centre of the node, where the plant's hormones are most concentrated. Remove shoots 10–13 cm (4–5 in) long with a heel from nonflowering half-ripe side shoots during mid to late summer. The best method I have found is to grip the side shoot in one hand near the union with the stem and grip the main shoot in the other, and pull downwards towards the roots, tearing the shoot away. Remove any excess wood, if present—very carefully cut it away in thin slices, a little at a time until there is something looking like an eye in the centre of the shield of bark. This is the heart of the node. With a sharp knife trim the length of torn bark and cambium to about 3 mm (0.1 in) below the union; this prevents the excess bark and wood from rotting and causing infection. Remove the lower leaves by rubbing them out with your thumb, which encourages secondary rooting up the stem. Leave only two to four upper leaves. If the upper leaves are large, trim them to reduce water loss. Dip the cutting in hormone rooting powder, tap off the excess, and insert in a rooting medium such as a 1:1 mix of peat and sharp sand. Either place the cuttings under a mist unit or line them out in a tightly covered cold frame. Alternatively, stand trays or pots in a propagating case or cover with clear plastic sheeting or a clear bag secured with an elastic band or raffia. The cuttings should root within three to four weeks.

Hardwood cuttings

By using hardwood cuttings, gardeners can reproduce the majority of *Buddleja* species and hybrids, including those of *B. davidii*. One of the major drawbacks of this technique is that it produces young plants with relatively few branches. In addition, the long distances between the nodes give the plant an overall leggy look, although this effect lessens with age. The best material for this method is the current year's growth without foliage—usually gathered from late autumn onwards. Use material about the thickness of a stout pencil. Cut at right angles to the stem about 5–10 mm (0.2–0.4 in) below a node to make a cutting roughly 25 cm (10 in) long. Rub out any side buds with your thumb up to the top 10 cm (4 in) of the cutting, as this will encourage rooting from the wounds. Cut the top end at 45° to identify the polarity of the cutting, so that it is inserted into the rooting medium the right way round. Dip the lower cut end into hormone rooting powder, tap off the excess, and insert the cutting in 1:1 peat and sharp sand mix or in open ground so that there is only the top 5–8 cm (2–3 in) showing. Repeat this exercise until you have 10 per cent over the required number, which should allow for any failures. Alternatively tie cuttings in bundles of ten and plunge them into a deep pot filled with sharp sand. Water well and leave to drain. Place the pot in a north-facing cold frame or unheated glasshouse protected from sudden rises in temperature. In the spring when the dormant side buds start to break, gently lift the cuttings out of the sand and pot up in John Innes no. 3.

Propagation Systems

The choice of a particular propagation system will depend on several factors. The costs of different materials, such as wood versus steel and glass, comes into play, as well as whether the space will be heated or unheated. Depending on the size of your garden or property, space may be an issue. Of course, the amount of time one has available to look after cuttings must be considered. Finally, the number of plants to be propagated will affect the choice of facilities. In fact, if only small quantities are needed, it may be less expensive to buy nursery-grown plants.

Warm bench and plastic

For bests results, this system should be set up in a glasshouse with warming cables on the bench. The bench is usually 0.6–0.9 m (2–3 ft) wide and the length of the glasshouse. It should be strong enough to hold 2.5–5 cm (1–2 in) of sand and have edges raised 5–10 cm (2 –4 in). A simple hooped framework erected over the bench will support the polythene covering. At the back of the bench the polythene should be buried into the edge of the sand to provide a good tight seal. Place the trays of cuttings under the polythene; pull the polythene sheeting taut and seal it. I find that lengths of wooden batons or metal rods hold the sheeting in place.

Cold frame

Semi-hardwood and hardwood cuttings can be inserted into a cold frame. These frames can be made of brick, concrete, wood, plastic, or metal, but must have a removable glass or Plexiglas cover set at an angle. Good dimensions for a cold frame are 15–23 cm (6–9 in) in front, 30–45 cm (12–18 in) at the back, and 0.9–1.2 m (3–4 ft) wide, with each cover panel equalling the width. Place the frame in a north-facing position away from the hottest sun. As the name implies, a cold frame does not include a source of heat, however you could install soil-warming cables. If temperatures drop below –5°C (24°F), cover the frame with a heavy blanket or fleece. Buddleja cuttings can be inserted directly into a sandy medium spread over in the base of the cold frame.

Low plastic tunnel

This system is suitable for hardwood and semi-hardwood cuttings. It is similar to the cold frame but it is constructed on the open ground. The site for this system needs to be carefully chosen, as a waterlogged site will not be suitable. In addition, the tunnel should be sited away from direct sunlight, especially afternoon sun. Beds are prepared by incorporating extra sand and peat into the soil. The soil mixture should be free-draining but retain enough moisture to keep the cuttings supplied with the correct amount of water. Insert the cuttings into the compost working from the front to the back. Label each batch of cuttings. Once the cuttings have been inserted the support hoops can be erected. You can buy low tunnels in kit form. Alternatively you can make your own using bamboo for the hoops and slipping them into sockets made of 2-cm (0.75-in) plastic water pipe cut into suitable lengths. Cover the hoops with clear polythene and tuck the edges securely into the soil. If temperatures drop below −5°C (24°F), cover the frame with a heavy blanket or fleece.

Open ground

Hardwood cuttings can be lined out into open ground in a sheltered part of the garden. This is probably the cheapest way to raise large numbers of plants suitable for large landscape plantings. A friend of mine wanted to have a 100-m-long hedge of *Buddleja* 'Clive Farrell'. He stuck cuttings directly into the prepared hedge line during late autumn, with a 95 per cent success rate. The gaps were easily filled in the following year. I do believe that this must be the longest buddleja hedge in Europe.

Dig a V-shaped trench to a depth of 20–25 cm (8–10 in) with a vertical back wall and the front cut in at about a 45° angle. Place sharp sand along the bottom of the trench so that the cuttings rest on it; this helps with rooting and reduces the risk of rotting. Place the cuttings with the square end on to the sand and backfill with soil. Firm in the row with your foot and label the cuttings. Allow the cuttings to develop over the year before lifting and planting out in their final place. I do not recommend potting up these rooted cuttings, as they are usually woody and leggy.

Micropropagation

The mass cloning of plants began in the early 1980s. Companies in the United States started mass-producing rhododendrons and other high-value shrubs, while Europeans focused on herbaceous perennials. Today a great many nurseries have their own micropropagation systems set up, churning out thousands of inexpensive cloned plantlets every year. *Buddleja* are very susceptible to eelworm damage, and they have become one of the major pests in the United States and Europe. Clean stock plants can be produced using micropropagation and tissue culture techniques. Micropropagation and tissue culture are similar to one another in that they use special agar (seaweed-based gelatine) preparations under sterile laboratory conditions. The main difference is the size of the material inserted into the agar. With tissue culture, meristematic tissue is liquefied down to small clusters of cells and spread on the agar surface. (Meristems are the parts of plants that are actively dividing; they are located in the apices of stems, shoots, and roots.) In micropropagation, small cuttings are inserted into the agar. These are specialist techniques requiring laboratory equipment and sterile conditions.

Chapter 5
Wildlife Attracted to Buddlejas

Buddleja flowers are best known for their perfume, which comes from the clear sugary nectar. It is because of this food source that butterflies and some other nectar-feeding wildlife are attracted to the flower spikes. The plants benefit from being well and truly pollinated by the attentive hungry visitors.

Moths and butterflies are both members of the insect order *Lepidoptera*. Although their caterpillars chew plant tissue, the adults mainly rely on a liquid diet full of energy-giving sugars. When butterflies and moths feed they unroll their proboscis, a feeding tube coiled up under the head when not in use. With their probosis they probe one flower after another searching out what little nectar there is available. Generally speaking, buddlejas are rather mean in the food-supply department and only release small quantities over a relatively long period. Thanks to this meanness, however, insects have to work hard to get a decent meal and we are able to enjoy their presence for a long period of time.

In this chapter I discuss various butterflies, moths, other insects, and birds that are known to visit and benefit buddleja plants, either by acting as pollinators or as predators of pest species. For a full list of buddleja pests, please refer to chapter 3.

Butterflies

Because of their size, colourful wings, and fascinating life cycle, butterflies have become the most common group of insects studied by hobbyists. The most striking feature of members of the *Lepidoptera* is the two pairs of membranous wings which are usually covered by a layer of overlapping scales (actually modified hairs). The majority of the more advanced species have a long spiral proboscis with which they suck up liquid nourishment. Lepidopterans metamorphose over the course of their life cycle, changing from larvae to pupae to winged adults. The larvae are commonly known as caterpillars and live on a variety of host plants—not necessarily the same nectar-producing flowering plants that attract the adult butterfly. Here I list some of the more common butterfly species visiting buddlejas. I thank the outstanding butterfly specialist Clive Farrell, proprietor of the Fallen Stones Butterfly Ranch in Belize, for giving me a better appreciation of these amazing insects.

Peacock butterfly (*Inachis io*)

This temperate Eurasian native is common in Britain and quite rare in North America. The peacock butterfly visits many garden plants, including *Buddleja*, and also feeds on sap flows, rotting fruits, and dung. The caterpillars feed on stinging nettles (*Urtica dioica*). The underside of the wings is covered in smoky brown to black hairs and scales, and the upper side of the wings is maroon with bold blue eyespots. This is a defence mechanism, intimidating predators such as birds into believing that the butterfly may in fact be a threat.

Marbled white (*Melanargia galathea*)

The marbled white is found in southern England and Western Europe. It has a very distinctive black and white pattern on its wings. It favours flower-rich grassy meadows, more often than not on chalk downlands. The caterpillars feed on grasses.

Eastern comma (*Polygonia comma*)

The eastern comma butterfly lives in deciduous woodlands near rivers, marshes, swamps, and other water sources. Its range is the eastern half of the United States, east of the Rocky Mountains from southern Canada to central Texas and the Gulf Coast. The adult's wing span is 4.5–6.4 cm (1.75–2.5 in). The forewing above is brownish orange with dark spots, with a dark spot at the centre of the bottom edge. The butterfly gets its name from the silver comma mark on the under surface of the wings, which is usually clubbed or hooked at both ends. The caterpillars feed on nettles

(*Urtica dioica*), hops (*Humulus lupulus*), and legumes such as alfalfa (*Medicago sativa*). In addition to flower nectar, the adults feed on rotting fruit and tree sap. The eastern comma can be found skipping through clearings, thickets, groves, and open woods typical of *Buddleja* country. This butterfly is very wary, darting rapidly away from any movement and frequently retreating into the shelter of the woods or shrubs.

Monarch butterfly (*Danaus plexippus*)

This is one of the most interesting North American butterflies. Over the course of a year, the monarch migrates vast distances. The migration occurs in huge numbers, and clouds of monarch butterflies are a common sight twice a year, in the spring and again in autumn. Its wintering grounds are along the southern California coast and in central Mexico; in summer monarchs range from southern Canada throughout the United States. At the Mexican wintering sites adults roost at night in trees, sometimes in aggregations of millions of butterflies.

The upper side of the adult's wings are orange with wide black borders and black veins. The fuzzy caterpillars are also orange and black. Both caterpillars and adults feed on milkweed (*Asclepias*), many of which contain poisonous cardiac glycosides. The monarchs store these distasteful poisons in their bodies. After tasting a monarch, a predator may associate the bright warning colours with an unpleasant meal and avoid them in the future. Before and after the milkweed blooming period, adult monarchs feed on the nectar of other flowering plants, including *Buddleja*.

Swallowtail (*Papilio machaon*)

On the hindwing near the tail, *Papilio machaon* has a distinctive reddish orange eyespot with black along the lower border. In North America, this Old World native ranges south from Alaska to northern British Columbia, east across Canada to Quebec, and from southern British Columbia south to New Mexico. *Papilio machaon* inhabits open hilltops, mountain meadows, and tundra. In the north the adults are active from late May to July.

The large, unmistakably beautiful butterfly is rare in Britain but more common in Europe; the European form occasionally migrates to the U.K. The upper side of the wings is creamy white with black veins with electric blue towards the rear. The caterpillars feed on members of the shrubby rose family (*Rosaceae*). In Europe the caterpillars feed on milk parsley (*Peucedanum palustre*), which is rare in Britain.

Pipevine swallowtail (*Battus philenor*)

This metallic blue North American swallowtail butterfly is stunning. The upper surface of the hindwing is iridescent blue or blue-green, and the underside has a row of seven round orange spots in an iridescent blue field. The wing span is 7–13 cm (2.8–5.2 in). Gardens have encouraged the spread and increase of this species by providing the adults with a plentiful supply of nectar from honeysuckle (*Lonicera*), swamp milkweed (*Asclepias curassavica*), orchids (*Dactylorhiza*), buddleja, lilac (*Syringia*), sweet rocket (*Hesperis matronalis*), and thistles (*Carduus, Onopordum*). The caterpillars feed on pipevine or Dutchman's pipe (*Aristolochia*), and Virginia snakeroot (*Aristolochia serpentaria*). The sap of Virginia snakeroot contains several complex toxins which the butterfly incorporates into its body. These give the pipevine swallowtail an unpleasant taste and provide protection against predators such as birds. Over time, many other swallowtails have evolved colouration similar to the pipevine to confuse predators. The technical term for this is Batesian mimicry. In the eastern United States and California, adults fly primarily in late spring and summer, but the pipevine swallowtail is more common in late summer and fall in the South and Southwest. In lowland tropical Mexico, adults may be found in any month.

Spicebush swallowtail (*Pterourus troilus*)

The spicebush swallowtail is easily identified by the large greenish blue spots along the outer border of the top surfaces of all four wings and the bright orange spot on the leading edge of each hindwing. Both sexes are blackish brown, and the wing span is 8.8–12.5 cm (3.5–5 in). The caterpillars feed on the spicebush (*Lindera benzoin*) and sassafras (*Sassafras albidum*), and adults feed on any good nectar source such as Buddleja, joe pye weed (*Eupatorium*), jewelweed (*Impatiens*), honeysuckle (*Lonicera*), and common milkweed (*Asclepias syriaca*) in gardens, woodland glades, orchards, road verges, and river banks. This butterfly ranges throughout the eastern United States from southern Canada to Florida, west to Oklahoma and central Texas; it occasionally strays to North Dakota, central Colorado, and Cuba. The adults of this species mimic the unpalatable pipevine swallowtail (*Battus philenor*). In addition, two large false eyes on the front end of the colourful caterpillar allow it to masquerade as a small lizard or snake, thereby discouraging attacks from predators. To further aid in its defence, the resting caterpillar avoids detection by hiding inside a rolled leaf shelter.

Eastern tiger swallowtail (*Papilio glaucus*)

To me, the eastern tiger swallowtail is one of the most beautiful of North American butterflies. The male is yellow with dark tiger stripes. Two forms of females exist: one is yellow like the male and the other is black with shadows of dark stripes. In both female forms the hindwing has many iridescent blue scales and an orange marginal spot; on the underside of the forewing the row of marginal spots merges into a continuous steely blue band. The wing span is 9.2–16.5 cm (3.7–6.6 in). The caterpillars feed on a wide range of broadleaved trees and shrubs. Adults feed in groups in gardens, woodland glades, orchards, road verges, and river banks. The eastern tiger swallowtail ranges from Ontario south to the Gulf Coast and west to the Colorado plains and central Texas.

White admiral (*Ladoga camilla*)

This species is a woodland dweller, but will venture into gardens if woods are nearby. It has a patchy distribution in southern England and a few sites in Wales, but is absent from Scotland and Ireland. The upper side of the wings is sooty black with white bands; the underside of the wings is a chestnut brown with similar white markings. The adults are often seen feeding on brambles (*Rubus*), and the caterpillars feed on honeysuckle (*Lonicera periclymenum*).

Red admiral (*Vanessa atalanta*)

This is one of the most common butterflies in Britain and is usually present from midsummer onwards. Though the red admiral does not usually survive the winter in the United Kingdom, summer migrants arrive in large numbers. In addition, this species ranges from Guatemala north through Mexico and the United States to northern Canada, and it is also found in New Zealand. Its preferred habitats are open sunny places where stinging nettles grow. The upper side of the wings is black with white spots near the apex; the forewing has a red band in the middle and the hindwing a red marginal band. The adults prefer to feed on sap flows, fermenting fruit, and bird droppings but visit flowers when these are not available. The caterpillars feed on members of the stinging nettle family (*Urticaceae*).

Painted lady (*Vanessa cardui*)

This is the most widely distributed butterfly in the world, being found on all continents except Australia and Antarctica. Occasionally, population explosions in Mexico cause massive migrations into the United States and Canada. The painted lady is a summer visitor to Britain and is usually found in meadows and other open or disturbed areas including gardens, old fields, and dunes. Adults prefer the nectar of composites, especially thistles (*Asteraceae*), although they visit a wide variety of nectar-producing plants, and I have frequently seen them feeding on *Buddleja*. The caterpillars feed on meadow plants, their favourites being thistles, stinging nettles and mallow (*Malvaceae*), and legumes (*Fabaceae*). The upper side of the wings is marbled with orange-brown and black. The forewing has a black apical patch and a white bar on the leading edge, and the hindwing has a row of five small black spots, sometimes with blue scales. The underside of the wings and main body parts are smoky brown. I find the painted lady difficult to tell apart from the small tortoiseshell, which can be distinguished by the blue fringe at the edge of its wings.

Small tortoiseshell (*Aglais urticae*)

The small tortoiseshell is common in the United Kingdom and ranges from Western Europe across the former Soviet Union to the Pacific Coast. It has been sighted twice in New York. This is a very common and familiar garden visitor in England, and small tortoiseshells can often be seen sunning themselves with wings wide open. The upper side of the wings is marbled orange-yellow and black, with a blue fringe at the edge of the wings. The underside of the wings and main body parts are smoky brown. Adults feed exclusively on flower nectar, and the caterpillars feed on stinging nettles (*Urticaceae*).

Orange sulphur (*Colias eurytheme*)

This species is also known as the alfalfa butterfly. The adult wing span is 3.5–7 cm (1.4–2.8 in). In males, the upper surface of the wing is yellow with an orange overlay, yellow veins, a wide black border, and dark black cell spot. Females are yellow or white with an irregular black border surrounding light spots. In both sexes, the underside of the hindwing has a silver spot with two concentric dark rings and a spot above it. The caterpillars feed almost exclusively on legumes and can easily be found eating alfalfa (*Medicago sativa*) and white clover (*Trifolium repens*). The orange sulphur has possibly the largest distribution range of all the North American butterflies, ranging from southern Canada to central Mexico, coast to coast in the United States except for the Florida peninsula. This butterfly inhabits a wide variety of open sites, especially clover and alfalfa fields, mowed fields, vacant lots, meadows, and road edges.

Cabbage white or large white (*Pieris brassicae*)

This butterfly is a common native in temperate Eurasia and has been noted rarely in North America. Adults are active in Europe and the United Kingdom from April through October, and they inhabit almost any open space. The underside of the wings is yellowish white, and the upper side of the wings is creamy white with black tips and several black dots on the forewings. Adults are nectar feeders, and the caterpillars feed on members of the cabbage family (*Brassicaceae*).

Small cabbage white or small white (*Pieris rapae*)

This butterfly is more common than the large white butterfly, but is smaller in size (wingspan 3.5–4 cm [1.5–1.75 in] versus 5–6 cm [2–2.5 in]). *Pieris rapae* is now found in temperate regions throughout the world. Like the large white, the underside of the wings is yellowish white and the upper side of the wings is creamy white with black tips on the forewings. The caterpillars feed on members of the cabbage family (*Brassicaceae*), such as broccoli, Brussels sprouts, cabbage, cauliflower, collard, and kale. Known as "cabbageworms," the caterpillars feed on foliage of these garden plants, and if left unchecked they may reduce mature plants to stems and leaf veins.

Moths

Several characteristics can be used to distinguish butterflies and moths. Most butterflies are brightly coloured, are active during the day, and have clubbed antennae, whereas most moths tend to be dull coloured and nocturnal and have tapered or feathery antennae. In addition, butterflies rest with their wings held vertically over their backs, whereas many moths fold their wings rooflike over their backs. Most adult moths are nectar feeders, although in the lower groups of moths some adults retain their larval mandibles and feed on pollen and spores.

Of the moths described here, the hummingbird hawk-moth and the silver Y moths are day fliers. The others are nocturnal, making it difficult to identify their habits after dark. The nocturnal moths described here are all known to frequent gardens after darkness, although other nocturnal moths undoubtedly feed on buddleja as well.

Hummingbird hawk-moth (*Macroglossum stellatarum*)

This moth has a wingspan of 45 mm (1.8 in). During long hot summers the Longstock collection was regularly visited by hummingbird hawk-moths. As the name suggests, this moth flies in much the same manner as a hummingbird, stopping only to extend its long proboscis to drink up the energy-giving nectar. This day-flying moth may be found in southern England as an occasional migrant from southern Europe, usually in the cooler hours of early morning and late afternoon. Apparently, this species has a fine memory, as individuals return to the same flowerbeds everyday at about the same time. The hummingbird hawk-moth is not native to Britain and seldom survives our winters. It breeds in the warmer parts of Europe and flies over the English Channel during the summer, hence the main summer sightings are in southern and eastern England. The hummingbird hawk-moth has a huge distribution throughout Europe, North Africa, and Asia, including India, China, Korea, and Japan.

Broad-bordered bee hawk-moth (*Hemaris fuciformis*)

This moth has a wingspan of 43 mm (1.7 in). The head and forewings are olive green, the middle of the forewings are transparent, and the edge is brown. When in flight, this moth has a striking resemblance to a large bumble-bee. *Hemaris fuciformis* is a day flier and is usually seen during the early summer hovering in front of flowers of plants such as *Buddleja alternifolia* and bugle (*Ajuga*). The broad-bordered bee hawk-moth generally avoids open meadows, preferring to fly along woodland margins. This moth breeds from Spain through Europe to the Ukraine. The larvae feed on honeysuckle (*Lonicera*). This an uncommon and very local woodland moth resident in southern England.

Silver Y moth (*Autographa gamma*)

The brownish yellow forewings of this moth are distinctively marked with a whitish silvery Y, and the hindwings are light brown. At rest, the moth is 23 mm (0.9 in) long. *Autographa gamma* is common in North Africa and the Mediterranean Basin during winter, and in summer it ranges as far north as Scotland and Finland. Under the right conditions, migrating swarms of these moths can be seen along the British coast in summer. The silver Y moth flies during the day during warm weather and visits garden flowers at dusk. I will always remember this moth in association with the cruel plant (*Araujia sericofera*). When the plant was in flower, the unsuspecting silver Y moths would feed on the nectar-rich flowers. The flowers, however, have a mechanism to hold the insect in place until the midday sun warmed up the flower parts, releasing the moth.

Poplar grey (*Acronicta megacephala*)

The forewings of the poplar grey are pale to dark grey and well marked with darker lines with a well-defined pale circle; the white hindwings have black veins. This moth is 20 mm (0.8 in) long at rest. The poplar grey is distributed throughout Western Europe, from Spain to the Arctic Circle. The adults are active from midspring to midsummer, and they prefer woodland habitats. These nocturnal moths are attracted to light and flowers and spend their days resting on tree trunks. The young feed on poplars (*Populus*) and willows (*Salix*).

Old lady (*Mormo maura*)

The forewings are a rich dark chocolate brown marked with scalloped lines, appearing like a shawl, hence the name "old lady." *Mormo maura* is a large, nocturnal species that prefers damp and wetland habitats, especially near wooded streams, river banks, and suburban gardens. In addition to flower nectar, the adults also feed on sap. The larvae feed on blackthorn (*Prunus spinosa*), hawthorn (*Crataegus monogyna*), willow (*Salix*), and birch (*Betula*). This moth has a widespread distribution in Western Europe, ranging as far north as The Netherlands and south to the Mediterranean.

Magpie (*Abraxas grossulariata*)

The forewings of the magpie moth are predominantly white with heavy black spotting, with a pale orange line near the margin. The hindwings are whiter with a row of black spots near the margin. *Abraxas grossulariata* is 38 mm (1.5 in) long at rest. This moth ranges throughout Europe and is found in woodlands, coastal dunes, and grasslands as well as gardens from early summer to early autumn. The caterpillars feed on gooseberries, currants, *Euonymus*, and some other shrubs.

Hebrew character (*Orthosia gothica*)

The pale purplish to greyish brown forewings are easily recognized by the dark mark in the middle of the wings, which has a transparent semicircle within it. The hindwings are brownish grey with a pale margin. This moth is 20 mm (0.8 in) long at rest. *Orthosia gothica* is common throughout Western Europe, north to the Arctic, in the spring. The young feed on a wide range of plants, including cultivated garden plants.

Lilac beauty (*Apeira syringaria*)

The lilac beauty moth is well camouflaged when at rest. A creased leading edge to the forewing and its yellow colour mottled with brown make the resting moth appear to be a dried, crumpled leaf. A reddish orange stripe spans the middle of the forewings. This moth has a wingspan of 40 mm (1.6 in) at rest. In Britain, it is active from early to midsummer. *Apeira syringaria* inhabits woodlands and hedgerows, and the larvae feed on honeysuckle (*Lonicera*) and privet (*Ligustrum*).

Brimstone moth (*Opisthographis luteolata*)

The brimstone moth is easily recognized by its bright yellow wings marked with chestnut blotches. It has a wingspan up to 38 mm (1.5 in). This woodland moth is present in most mature gardens throughout Britain, being active from spring to late summer. Although adults can often be seen flying during daylight hours, the brimstone moth is most likely to be seen around dusk. The larvae feed on blackthorn (*Prunus spinosa*), hawthorn (*Crataegus monogyna*), and other shrubs in the rose family.

Other Animals

Although *Buddleja* are commonly known as "butterfly bushes," if you are patient it will be surprising who else visits this remarkable genus, especially when the bushes are in flower.

Hummingbirds (*Trochilidae*)

I saw my first hummingbird in San Francisco, darting from one buddleja flower to another. I was so excited to see one up close, as until then I had only seen them in zoos. My second sighting in the wild was during a trip into the jungles of Belize, Guatemala, and Mexico. The birds were like flashes of colour as they passed by in a blur of iridescent green; it was not until they momentarily stopped to feed on a flower that they came into focus.

Hummingbirds feed primarily on the nectar of flowers and supplement their diet with small insects. They have evolved narrow elongated beaks, extendable tongues, and hovering flight, all of which allow them to exploit nectar resources. Hummingbird-pollinated flowers are usually brightly coloured and scentless and have long, tubular corollas. Because hummingbirds have a high metabolic rate, they can drink their body mass in nectar in less than a day (most species weight between 2.5 and 6.5 g [0.09–0.23 oz]).

Hummingbirds are found only in the New World. Their range extends from Alaska to Labrador in the north to Tierra del Fuego in the south and from Barbados to the Juan Fernandes Islands. Most species are tropical and subtropical. Hummingbirds feed and nest in a wide variety of habitats, both temperate and tropical; the main habitat requirement for hummingbirds is a large number of nectar-producing flowers. Due to the prevalence of hummingbird feeders and cultivated gardens, hummingbirds can also be found in urban and suburban areas with few natural food sources.

Common wasp (*Vespula vulgaris*) and European hornet (*Vespa crabro*)

Vespula vulgaris is known as the yellowjacket in the United States. As the common name implies, the hornet *Vespa crabro* is native to central and Western Europe, but this species is also found in south-eastern Canada and throughout much of the eastern United States as far west as Michigan. Although the sting from a wasp or hornet can be very painful to humans, these insects are usually mild mannered and not prone to attack unless their nests are disturbed. These predacious insects are active from the early months of the year up to late summer. Wasps and hornets feed on insect pests, and can be seen searching for victims feeding on flowers such as buddleja.

Ladybird beetle (*Coccinellidae*)

Ladybird beetles, lady beetles, or ladybugs are among the most visible and best known beneficial predatory insects. Adults are usually red or orange with black spots, although some ladybird beetles are black, often with red markings, or yellow with black spots. The larvae are greyish black and resemble alligators with three pairs of legs. Ladybird beetles overwinter as adults, often in aggregations along hedgerows, beneath leaf litter, under rocks and bark, and in other protected places, including buildings. The females lay eggs only where aphids are present. Both the adults and larvae feed primarily on aphids; when aphids are scarce, however, they will also eat mites, scales, insect eggs, pollen, and nectar. Both adults and larvae live on plants frequented by aphids, including roses, oleander, milkweed, and broccoli. I have seen ladybird beetles in numbers on the buddleja collection.

Common green lacewing (*Chrysopa carnea*)

Green lacewings are common in much of North America, Europe, and the British Isles. Adult green lacewings are pale green, about 12–20 mm (0.5–0.8 in) long, with long antennae, bright golden eyes, large transparent wings, and a slender body. They are active fliers, particularly at night, and have a characteristic fluttering flight. This species of green lacewings over-winter as adults, usually in outbuildings and other sheltered places. During the spring and summer, females lay several hundred small eggs on leaves or twigs in the vicinity of prey. Adults feed only on nectar, pollen, and aphid honeydew, but their larvae are active aphid predators and are sometimes called "aphid lions." In addition to aphids, they also feed on spider mites (especially red mites); thrips; whiteflies; eggs of leafhoppers, moths, and leafminers; small caterpillars; beetle larvae; and tobacco budworm.

Where to See Buddlejas

The gardeners of the United Kingdom have a long and unique history of collecting plants from all over the world, from which they have bred a wide range of beautiful and economically important cultivars. Over the years many professional gardeners have had a favourite plant species or cultivar which they are passionate about; naturally they want to learn all about them by collecting books and articles as well as by building a living collection in their garden or place of work. Sadly many of these original plants have been lost or are rapidly disappearing from culture.

In an effort to remedy these trends, in 1978 The National Council for the Conservation of Plants and Gardens was established. The mission statement of the council is to "conserve endangered plants by cultivating them in parks, gardens and arboreta," and its formal objectives are to define rarity of horticultural plants so that those in danger of being lost to cultivation can be saved; to list gardens containing important plantings or representing a particular style so that the benefit of these to the community can be retained; and to establish definitive collections of specific genera (held under the National Collection scheme) to provide a source of propagating material and opportunities for research and education.

Throughout the United Kingdom local groups have been set up to support the work of the collection holders and private individuals who share a common interest in plants. The main function of the groups is to promote public awareness of the activity of the National Council for the Conservation of Plants and Gardens. The groups arrange several activities throughout the year, varying from plant sales and garden visits to lectures, workshops, and master classes from collection holders. The main web page of the National Council for the Conservation of Plants and Gardens (www.nccpg.com) is a good source of horticultural and tourist information for keen plantspeople. Many local groups have their own web pages, usually listing the collection holders' information, activities, and contact addresses.

The gardens listed in this appendix have a wide range of *Buddleja* species in a variety of displays. In the United Kingdom, the national collections of the genus can be seen at Paignton Zoo, The Lavender Garden, Tetbury, and at Longstock Park Gardens. In the United States, Mike Dirr at the University of Georgia–Athens, Bernheim Arboretum, and Longwood Gardens each have amassed a vast collection of *Buddleja* for scientific evaluation.

United Kingdom

Abbotsbury Sub-Tropical Gardens
Abbotsbury
Weymouth
Dorset DT3 4LA
(01305) 871344

Barnsdale Gardens
Exton Avenue
Exton
Oakham
Rutland LE15 8AH
(01572) 813200

The Beth Chatto Gardens Ltd
Elmstead Market
Colchester
Essex CO7 7DB
(01206) 822007

Bluebell Arboretum and Nursery
Annwell Lane
Smisby
Ashby de la Zouch
Derbyshire LE65 2TA
(01530) 413700

Bodnant Garden
Tal-y-cafn
Colway Bay
Clwyd LL28 5RE
Wales
(01492) 650731

Cally Gardens
Gatehouse of Fleet
Castle Douglas DG7 2DJ
Scotland
(01557) 815029

Crûg Farm Plants
Griffith's Crossing
Caernarfon, Gwynedd
LL55 1TU
Wales
(01248) 670232

Great Dixter
Northiam
Rye
East Sussex TN31 6PH
(01797) 253107

The Herb Garden and Historical Plant Nursery Centre
Pentre Berw
Gaerwen
Anglesey LL60 6LF
(01248) 422208

The Lavender Garden
Ashcroft
Ozleworth
Kingscote
Tetbury
Gloucestershire GL8 8YF
(01453) 860356

Longstock Park Nursery
Longstock
Stockbridge
Hampshire SO20 6EH
(01264) 810894

Paignton Zoo
Totnes Road
Paignton
Devon TQ4 7EU
(01803) 697500

Royal Horticultural Society's Garden Wisley
Wisley
Woking
Surrey GU23 6QB
(01483) 211113

Sherwood House and Cottage Nursery
Newton St Cyres
Sherborne
Devon EX5 5BT
(01392) 851589

Ventnor Botanic Garden
Undercliff Drive
Ventnor
Isle of Wight PO38 1UL
(01983) 855397

North America

Bernheim Arboretum and Research Forest
State Highway 245
P.O. Box 139
Clermont, Kentucky 40110
502-955-8512

Carroll Gardens
444 East Main Street
Westminster, Maryland 21157
800-638-6334

Fairweather Gardens
PO Box 330
Greenwich, New Jersey 08323
609-451-6261

Forestfarm
990 Tetherow Road
Williams, Oregon 97544
541-846-7269

Greer Gardens
1280 Goodpasture Island Road
Eugene, Oregon 97401
541-686-8266

Kartuz Greenhouses
P.O. Box 790
1408 Sunset Drive
Vista, California 92085-0790
760-941-3613

Longwood Gardens
Route 1
P.O. Box 501
Kennett Square, Pennsylvania 19348-0501
610-388-1000

Niche Gardens
1111 Dawson Road
Chapel Hill, North Carolina 27516
919-967-0078

The Plant Farm
177 Vesuvius Road
Salt Spring Island
British Columbia V8K 1K3
Canada
025-053-75995

University of Georgia–Athens
Department of Horticulture
1111 Plant Sciences Building
Athens, Georgia 30602
706-542-2471

Austria

Praskac Pflanzenland
Praskackstraße 101-108
3430 Tullen
Donau
022-726-2460

Belgium

Arboretum Waasland
Kriekelaarstraat 29
9100 Nieuwkerken
Waas
037-759-309

Plantkundige Kwekerij
Iepersesteenweg 112
8630 Veurne
058-313-335

France

André Briant Jeunes Plants
La Bouvinerie
BP 15
49180 Saint Barthélémy
d'Anjou Cedex
024-193-9286

Les Jardins de Cotelle
76370 Derchigny
Graincourt
023-583-6138

Les Jardins de la Brande
La Brande
24380 Fouliex
055-307-4785

Germany

Der Bamberger Staudengarten
Gundelsheimer Straße 80
96052 Bamberg
095-162-242

Friesland Staudengarten
Husumar Weg 16
26441 Jever
Rahrdum
044-613-763

Gärtengestaltung und Imkerei
Allerfeld Straße 9
31832 Springe
050-458-383

Gärtnerei Baumschule
Alte Zoll Straße 18
77694 Kehl
078-512-583

Pflanzenhandel
Maldfeld Straße 4
Marmstorf
21077 Hamburg
040-761-080

Soltaur Baumschulen
Wiedinger Weg 12
29614 Soltau
051-913-450

Versandbaumschule
Kieler Straße 5
25474 Hasloh
041-062-031

Italy

Fratelli Margheriti
Monte San Paolo 50
53043 Chiusi
Siena
057-822-7686

Montivivai
Via per Picciorana
55010 Tempagno
Lucca
058-399-8115

Vivai Fratelli Tusi s.d.f.
Via Sorbara 38
46013 Canneto sull'Oglio MN
037-672-3460

Vivaio Luciano Noaro
Via Vittorio e Manuele 151
18033 Camporosso IM
018-428-8225

The Netherlands

Baumschulen Pieter Zwijnenburg
Halve Raak 18
2771 AD
Boskoop
017-221-6232

Bulkyard Plants
Postbus 56
2770 AB
Boskoop
017-221-0743

Hanno Hardyzer
Laag Boskoop 112
2771 HA
Boskoop
017-221-5705

Switzerland

Staudengärtnerei
Longin Ziegler
Oberzelg
8627 Grüningen
019-351-383

Where to Buy Buddlejas

United Kingdom

Abbotsbury Sub-Tropical Gardens
Abbotsbury
Weymouth
Dorset DT3 4LA
(01305) 871344

Barncroft Nurseries
Dunwood Lane
Longsdon
Leek
Stoke-on-Trent ST9 9QW
(01538) 384310

Barnsdale Gardens
Exton Avenue
Exton
Oakham
Rutland LE15 8AH
(01572) 813200

Beacon's Botanicals
Banc-y-Felin
Carregsawdde
Llangadog
Carmarthenshire SA19 9DA
Wales
(01550) 777992

The Beth Chatto Gardens
Elmstead Market
Colchester
Essex CO7 7DB
(01206) 822007

Bluebell Arboretum and Nursery
Annwell Lane
Smisby
Ashby-de-la-Zouch
Derbyshire LE65 2TA
(01530) 413700

Bodiam Nursery
Cowfield Cottage
Bodiam
Robertsbridge
East Sussex TN32 5RA
(01580) 830811

Bodnant Garden Nursery Ltd.
Tal-y-cafn
Colway Bay
Clwyd LL28 5RE
Wales
(01492) 650731

Bonhard Nursery
Murrayshall Road
Scone
Perth PH2 7PQ
Scotland
(01738) 552791

The Botanic Nursery
Bath Road
Atworth
Melksham
Wiltshire SN12 8NU
(07850) 328756

Bridgemere Nursery
Bridgemere
Nantwich
Cheshire CW5 7QB
(01270) 521100

Broadstone Nurseries
The Nursery
13 High Street
Abington
Oxfordshire OX14 4UA
(01235) 847557

Buckerfield Nursery
Ogbourne St. George
Marlborough
Wiltshire SN8 1SG
(01672) 841065

Buckingham Nurseries
14 Tingewick Road
Buckingham
Buckinghamshire MK18 4AE
(01280) 822133

Burncoose Nurseries
Gwennap
Redruth
Cornwall TR16 6BJ
(01209) 860316

Cally Gardens
Gatehouse of Fleet
Castle Douglas DG7 2DJ
Scotland
(01557) 815029

Collector's Corner Plants
33 Rugby Road
Rugby
Warwickshire CV23 0DE
(01788) 571881

Compton Lane Nurseries
Little Compton
Moreton-in-Marsh
Gloucestershire GL56 0SJ
(01608) 674578

Cottage Nurseries
Thoresthorpe
Alford
Lincolnshire LN13 0HX
(01507) 466968

Crûg Farm Plants
Caernarfon
Gwynedd
LL55 1TU
Wales
(01248) 670232

Eildon Plants
Melrose
Roxburghshire TD6 9BJ
Scotland
(01896) 755530

Fillpots Nursery
52 Straight Road
Boxted
Colchester
Essex CO4 5RB
(01206) 272389

Ford Nursery
Castle Gardens
Ford
Berwick-upon-Tweed TD15 2PZ
(01890) 820379

Garden Plants
Windy Ridge
Victory Road
St. Margarets-at-Cliffe
Dover
Kent CT15 6HF
(01304) 853225

Goscote Nurseries Ltd
Syston Road
Cossington
Leicestershire LE7 4UZ
(01509) 812121

Great Dixter Nurseries
Northiam
Rye
East Sussex TN31 6PH
(01797) 253107

**The Herb Garden and Historical
Plant Nursery Centre**
Berw
Gaerwen
Anglesey LL60 6LF
(01248) 422208

Hopley's Plants Ltd
High Street
Much Hadham
Hertfordshire SG10 6BU
(01279) 842509

Hortus Nursery
Shrubbery Bungalow
School Lane
Rousdon
Lyme Regis
Dorset DT7 3XW
(01297) 444019

The Lavender Garden
Ashcroft Nurseries
Ozleworth
Kingscote
Tetbury
Gloucestershire GL8 8YF
(01453) 860356

**The Longframlington Centre for
Plants and Gardens**
Swarland Road
Morpeth
Northumberland NE65 8DB
(01655) 703282

Longstock Park Nursery
Longstock
Stockbridge
Hampshire SO20 6EH
(01264) 810894

Macpenny's Nurseries
154 Burley Road
Bransgore
Christchurch
Dorset BH23 8DB
(01425) 673948

Norwell Nurseries
Woodhouse Road
Norwell
Newark
Nottinghamshire NG23 6JX
(01636) 636337

The Walled Garden
Frampton-on-Severn
Gloucestershire
GL2 7EX
(01452) 741641

The Old Walled Garden
Oxonhoath
Hadlow
Kent TN11 9SS
(01732) 810012

Pan-Global Plants
The Walled Garden
Frampton Court
Frampton-on-Severn
Gloucestershire GL2 7EX
(01452) 741641

Perhill Nurseries
Worcester Road
Great Witley
Worcestershire WR6 6JT
(01299) 896329

Perryhill Nurseries Ltd
Hartfield
East Sussex TN7 4JP
(01892) 770377

Perry's Plants
The River Garden
Sleights
Whitby
North Yorkshire YO21 1RR
(01947) 810329

The Plantsman Nursery
North Wonson Farm
Throwleigh
Okehampton
Devon EX20 2JA
(01647) 231699

Sampford Shrubs
Sampford Peverell
Tiverton
Devon EX16 7EN
(01884) 821164
www.samshrub.co.uk

Sherwood Cottage Nursery
Newton St Cyres
Sherborne
Devon EX5 5BT
(01392) 851589

Spinners Nursery
School Lane
Boldre
Lymington
Hampshire SO41 5QE
(01590) 673347

Ventnor Botanic Garden
Undercliff Drive
Ventnor
Isle of Wight PO38 1UL
(01983) 855397

Wallace Plants
Lewes Road Nursery
Lewes Road
Laughton
East Sussex BN8 6BN
(01323) 811729

Waterperry Gardens Ltd
Waterperry
Wheatley
Oxfordshire OX33 1JZ
(01844) 339226

Webbs of Wychbold
Wychbold
Droitwich
Worcestershire WR9 0DG
(01527) 861777

W. E. Ingwersen Ltd
Birch Farm Nursery
Gravetye
East Grinstead
West Sussex RH19 4LE
(01342) 810236

West Acre Gardens
West Acre
King's Lynn
Norfolk PE32 1UJ
(01760) 755562

Wisley Plant Centre (RHS)
Royal Horticultural Society's
Garden Wisley
Woking
Surrey GU23 6QB
(01483) 211113

North America

Carroll Gardens
444 East Main Street
Westminster, Maryland 21157
800-638-6334
www.carrollgardens.com

Fairweather Gardens
P.O. Box 330
Greenwich, New Jersey 08323
609-451-6261

Forestfarm
990 Tetherow Road
Williams, Oregon 97544
541-846-7269

Greene Hill Nursery
5027 Highway 147 N
Waverly, Alabama 36879
334-864-7500
www.greenehill.com

Greer Gardens
Harold Greer
1280 Goodpasture Island Road
Eugene, Oregon 97401
541-686-8266

Herronswood Nursery Ltd.
7530 NE 288th Street
Kingston, Washington 98346
360-297-4172

Hines Nursery
333 Cypress Run
Houston, Texas 77094
281-675-1600

Joy Creek Nursery
20300 NW Watson Road
Scappoose, Oregon 97056
503-543-7474

Kartuz Greenhouses
P.O. Box 790
1408 Sunset Drive
Vista, California 92085
760-941-3613

Louisiana Nursery
5853 Highway 182
Opelousas, Louisiana 70570
318-948-3696

Mountain Valley Growers
38325 Pepperweed Road
Squaw Valley, California 93675
559-338-2775
www.mountainvalleygrowers.com

Niche Gardens
Kim Hawks
1111 Dawson Road
Chapel Hill, North Carolina 27516
919-967-0078

Pike Family Nurseries
4020 Steve Reynolds Blvd.
Norcross, Georgia 30093
770-921-1022
www.pikenursery.com

Plant Delights Nursery
9241 Sauls Road
Raleigh, North Carolina 27603
919-772-4794

The Plant Farm
177 Vesuvius Road
Salt Spring Island
British Columbia V8K 1K3
Canada
250-537-5995

Rice Creek Gardens, Inc.
11506 Highway 65
Blaine, Minnesota 55434
612-754-8090
www.ricecreekgardens.com

Sandy Mush Herb Nursery
316 Suret Cove Road
Leicester, North Carolina 28748
826-683-2014

Southern Perennials and Herbs
98 Bridges Road
Tylertown, Mississippi 39667
601-684-1769

Spring Meadow Nursery
12601 120th Avenue
Grand Haven, Michigan 49417
616-846-4729
www.pottedliners.com/

Weisse Brothers Nursery
11690 Colfax Highway
Grass Valley, California 95945
530-272-7657

Austria

Praskac Pflanzenland
Praskackstraße 101-108
3430 Tullen
Donau
022-726-2460

Belgium

Arboretum Waasland
Kriekelaarstraat 29
9100 Nieuwkerken
Waas
037-759-309

Plantkundige Kwekerij
Iepersesteenweg 112
8630 Veurne
058-313-335

France

André Briant Jeunes Plants
La Bouvinerie
BP 15
49180 Saint Barthélémy
d'Anjou Cedex
024-193-9286

Earl Pépinières Botaniques
Allée du Marquis
22200 Graces
Guingamp
029-644-4616

Fragrance
La Jugnon
71800 Vauban
038-525-8958

Les Jardins de Cotelle
76370 Derchigny
Graincourt
023-583-6138

Les Jardins de la Brande
La Brande
24380 Fouliex
055-307-4785

Les Pépinière délle Normandie
15 Le Repas
50680 Villiers
Fossard
023-305-8864

Pépinières d'Argonne
Route de Varennes
55120 Clermont-en-Argonne
032-988-4634

Pépinières de Bernay
Menneval
27300 Bernay
023-243-0778

Pépinières du Mas de Quinty
30440 Roquedur
046-782-4531

Pépinières La Forêt
BP 32
44840 Les-Sorinières
024-004-4203

Pépinières Michaud
Rue de l'Audonnerie
79240 L'Absie
054-995-8012

Pépinières Renault
Domaine du Rocher
53120 Gorron
024-308-6045

Pépinières Thuilleaux
6 route de Rambouillet
78460 Choisel
013-052-3616

SA Pépinières Jumentier
l avenue de l'Etang
49123 Ingrandes-sur-Loire
024-139-2722

SA Pépinières Plandanjou
Avenue Admiral Chauvin
BP 62
49136 Les-Ponts-de-Ce
024-179-4480

Germany

Baumschulen Peter Kessler
Eiseohr Straße 6
79664 Wehr
077-628-319

Baumschulen Wilhelm Müller
Paul-Lincke-Weg 2
69245 Bammental
062-234-0637

Der Bamberger Staudengarten
Gundelsheimer Straße 80
96052 Bamberg
095-162-242

Friesland Staudengarten
Husumar Weg 16
26441 Jever
Rahrdum
044-613-763

Gärtengestaltung und Imkerei
Allerfeld Straße 9
31832 Springe
050-458-383

Gärtnerei Baumschule
Alte Zoll Straße 18
77694 Kehl
078-512-583

Pflanzenhandel
Maldfeld Straße 4
Marmstorf
21077 Hamburg
040-761-080

Soltaur Baumschulen
Wiedinger Weg 12
29614 Soltau
051-913-450

Versandbaumschule
Kieler Straße 5
25474 Hasloh
041-062-031

Italy

Fratelli Margheriti
Monte San Paolo 50
53043 Chiusi
Siena
057-822-7686

Montivivai
Via per Picciorana
55010 Tempagno
Lucca
058-399-8115

Vivai Fratelli Tusi s.d.f.
Via Sorbara 38
46013 Canneto sull'Oglio MN
037-672-3460

Vivaio Luciano Noaro
Via Vittorio e Manuele 151
18033 Camporosso IM
018-428-8225

The Netherlands

Baumschulen Pieter Zwijnenburg
Halve Raak 18
2771 AD
Boskoop
017-221-6232

Bulkyard Plants
Postbus 56
2770 AB
Boskoop
017-221-0743

Hanno Hardyzer
Laag Boskoop 112
2771 HA
Boskoop
017-221-5705

Switzerland

Baumschulen Otto Eisenhut
6575 San Nazarro
Tessin
091-795-1867

Staudengärtnerei
Longin Ziegler
Oberzelg
8627 Grüningen
019-351-383

Bibliography

Arnold, T. H., and B. C. de Wet. 1993. *Plants of Southern Africa: Names and Distribution.* National Botanical Institute of South Africa, Pretoria.

Bean, W. J. 1950. *Trees and Shrubs Hardy in the British Isles.* John Murray, London.

Bentham, G. 1861. *Flora Hong Kongensis.* L. Reeve, London.

Bonpland, A. J. A. 1818. *Nova Genera et Species Plantarum.* Pp. 351–352. Lutetiae Parisiorum, Paris.

Brickell, Christopher, ed. 1989. *The Royal Horticultural Society Encyclopedia of Garden Plants and Flowers.* Dorling Kindersley, London.

Brummitt. R. K. 1912. *Vascular Plant Families and Genera.* Royal Botanic Gardens, Kew.

Burtt, B. L. 1939. *Buddleja fallowiana. Botanical Magazine* 162: 9564

Catchpole, N. 1963. *Flowering Shrubs and Trees.* W. H. & L. Collingridge, London.

Ching, Pei. 1985. *Flora Yunnanica.* Fahsing Publishing, Shanghai.

Coates, P., M. Coates, and K. Palgrave. 1988. *Trees of Southern Africa.* Central News Agency, Johannesburg.

Compton, J. 1984. *Buddleja bhutanica. The Garden* 109(2): 83.

Coombes, A. J. 2001. *The Illustrated Encyclopedia of Trees and Shrubs.* Salamander Books, London.

Cotton, A. D. 1947. Spring-flowering buddleias. *Journal of the Royal Horticultural Society* 72: 427–435

Cox, E. H., and P. A. Cox. 1958. *Modern Shrubs.* Thomas Nelson & Sons, London.

Daydon, B. J. 2004. A *Glossary of Botanical Terms.* Asiatic Publishers, Delhi, India.

Desmond, Ray. 1994. *Dictionary of British and Irish Botanists and Horticulturists.* Taylor & Francis Ltd., London.

Dirr, Michael. 1975. *Manual of Woody Landscape Plants.* Stipes Publishing, Champaign, Illinois.

Dirr, Michael. 1978. *Manual of Woody Plants.* Stipes Publishing, Champaign, Illinois.

Everett, T. H. 1981. *The New York Botanical Garden Illustrated Encyclopedia of Horticulture.* Garland, New York.

Gunther, Robert, ed. 1928. *Further Correspondence of John Ray.* Ray Society, London.

Hayashi, Y. 1985. *Woody Plants of Japan.* YAMA-Kei, Tokyo.

Hellyer, Arthur. 1982. *The Collingridge Illustrated Encyclopedia of Gardening.* Collingridge Books, London.

Hillier, John. 1993. *The Hillier Manual of Trees and Shrubs.* 6th ed. David & Charles, London.

Hooker, J. D. 1895. *Buddleja colvilei. Botanical Magazine* 121: 7449.

Hooker, J. D. 1898. *Buddleja davidii. Botanical Magazine* 124: 7609.

Hooker, J. W. 1828. *Buddleja madagascariensis. Botanical Magazine* 55: 2824.

Huxley, A., M. Griffiths, and M. Levy, eds. 1992. *The New RHS Dictionary of Gardening.* Macmillan, London.

Hyams, Edward. 1966. *Ornamental Shrubs for Temperate Zone Gardeners.* Vol. 4. Thames and Hudson, London.

Joffe, P. 2001. *Creative Gardening with Indigenous Plants.* Briza Publications, Pretoria.

Kearney, T. H., and R. H. Peebles. 1942. *Flowering Plants and Ferns of Arizona.* Misc. Publ. 423. U.S. Department of Agriculture, Washington, D.C.

Kelly, J., and J. Hillier. 1995. *Hillier's Garden Guide to Trees and Shrubs.* David & Charles, England.

Krüssmann, G. 1984. *Manual of Cultivated Broad-leaved Trees and Shrubs.* Timber Press, Portland, Oregon.

L. H. Bailey Hortorium. 1976. *Hortus Third: A Concise Dictionary of Plants Cultivated in the USA and Canada.* Macmillan, New York.

Lamb, J. G. D., J. C. Kelly, and P. Bowbrick. 1975. *Nursery Stock Manual.* Pitman Press, Bath, England.

Leeuwenberg, A. J. M. 1979. *The Loganiaceae of Africa.* Vol. 18. Veenman H. & Zonen B.V., Wageningen, The Netherlands.

Leistner, O. A. 2000. *Seed Plants of South Africa.* National Botanical Institute, Pretoria.

Mabberley, D. J. 1997. *The Plant Book.* Cambridge University Press.

Macbride, J. F. 1950. Flora of Peru. *Field Museum of Natural History–Botany* 13(3): 239–249.

Macoboy, Stirling. 1989. *What Shrub is That?* P. 65. Weldon Publishing, Sydney.

Marquand, C. V. B. 1930. Revision of the Old World *Buddleja. Royal Botanic Garden Kew Bulletin* 1930: 177–208.

Maunder, Michael. 1987. Notes on tender species of *Buddleja. The Plantsman* 9: 65–80.

Meakin, J., and B. N. Peterson. 1996. *Plants That Merit Attention.* Vol. 11. *Shrubs.* The Garden Club of America and Timber Press, Portland, Oregon.

Nashir, E. 1974. *Flora of Pakistan.* No. 56. Stewart Herbarium, Gordon College, Rawalpindi, Pakistan.

Nicholson, George. 1884. *The Illustrated Dictionary of Gardening.* Bradley, London.

Norman, Eliane Meyer. 1981. *Buddleja nappii. Botanical Magazine* 183, table 807.

Norman, Eliane Meyer. 1982. *Flora of Ecuador.* No. 16. University of Göteborg, Swedish Research Council Publishing House.

Norman, Eliane Meyer. 2000. *Flora Neotropica.* Pp. 1–171, *Buddlejaceae.* New York Botanical Garden, New York.

Norman, Eliane Meyer. 2000. *Organization for Flora Neotropica.* New York Botanical Garden, New York.

Norman, Eliane Meyer. 1966. *The Genus Buddleja in North America.* New York Botanical Garden, New York.

Palmer, E., and N. Pitman. 1972. *Trees of Southern Africa.* Balkema Publishing, Cape Town.

Philips, R., and M. Rix. 1989. *Shrubs.* Pp. 208–211. Pan Books Ltd., London.

Ping-tao, Li, and P. H. Raven. 1996. *Flora of China.* Vol. 15. Missouri Botanical Garden Science Press, Beijing.

Pollok, M., and M. Griffith. 1998. *The RHS Shorter Dictionary of Gardening.* Macmillan, London.

Pooley, Elsa. 1993. *The Complete Field Guide to Trees of Natal, Zululand and Transkei.* Natal Flora Publications Trust, Durban, South Africa.

Richardson, J. E. 2000. *The European Garden Flora.* Vol. 6. Cambridge University Press, Cambridge.

Rodriguez, R. 1983. *Flora Arborea de Chile.* P. 345. Editorial de la Universidad Santiago, Santiago.

Royal Horticultural Society. 2003. *RHS Plant Finder 2004–2005.* Dorling Kindersley, London.

Sanso, A. M., and C. C. Xifreda. 1999. *Catálogo de las Plantas vasculares da la Republica Argentina.* Missouri Botanical Garden Press, St. Louis.

Sealy, A. 1950. *Buddleja forrestii. Botanical Magazine* 167: 93.

Standley, P. C. 1924. *Trees and Shrubs of Mexico.* Smithsonian Institute, Washington, D.C.

Standley, P. C. 1938. Flora of Costa Rica. *Field Museum of Natural History–Botany* 18(3): 920–921.

Stapf, Otto. 1925–1926. *Buddleja alternifolia. Botanical Magazine* 151: 9085.

Stephen, Leslie. 1886. *Dictionary of National Biography.* Vol. 7. Smith Elder & Co., London.

Steward, A. N. 1958. *Vascular Plants of the Lower Yangtze.* Oregon State College, Corvallis.

Stierlin, Henri. 2001. *The Maya Architecture of the World.* Compagnie du Livre d'Art SA, Lusanne.

Synge, Patrick. M., ed. 1956. *Royal Horticultural Society Dictionary of Gardening.* 2nd ed. Clarendon Press, Oxford.

Thomas, Graham Stuart. 1992. *Ornamental Shrubs, Climbers, and Bamboos.* J. M. Dent Ltd., London.

Thomas, V. and R. Grant. 1998. *Tree Spotting in Highveld and the Drakensberg.* Jacana Publishers, Houghton, South Africa.

Van Wyk, B., and P. Van Wyk. 1997. *Field Guide to the Trees of South Africa.* Struik, Cape Town.

Venter, F., and J.-A. Venter. 1996. *Making the Most of Indigenous Trees.* Briza Publications, Arcadia, South Africa.

Von Humboldt, F. W. H. A. 1818. *De distributione geographica secundum coeli temperiem et altidudinem montium.* Nov. gen. sp. 2: 280 folio. Lutetiae Parisiopum, Paris.

Wright, C. H. 1911. *Buddleja officinalis. Botanical Magazine* 137: 8401.

Yamazaki, T., and D. E. Boufford. 1993. *Flora of Japan.* Vol. 111a. Kodansha Publishing, Tokyo.

Index